i'm going to break your heart

I'm Going to Break Your Heart

a rock n roll
love story

Chantal Kreviazuk
& Raine Maida

ECW

Published by ECW Press
665 Gerrard Street East
Toronto, Ontario, Canada M4M 1Y2
416-694-3348 / info@ecwpress.com

CERTIFIED CANADIAN PUBLISHER

Editor for the Press: Michael Holmes
Story Editor: Hayley Gene Penner
Cover design: Jessica Albert
Cover photo: Kat Nijmeddin
Interior design and typesetting: Troy Cunningham

To the best of their abilities, the authors have related experiences, places, people, and organizations from their memories of them. In order to protect the privacy of others, they have, in some instances, changed the names of certain people and details of events and places.

Unless otherwise specified, all photos are from the authors' personal collection. The publishers would be glad to amend in future editions any errors or omissions brought to their attention

LIBRARY AND ARCHIVES CANADA CATALOGUING IN PUBLICATION

Title: I'm going to break your heart : a rock n roll love story / Chantal Kreviazuk & Raine Maida.
Other titles: I am going to break your heart
Names: Kreviazuk, Chantal, 1974- author | Maida, Raine, author.
Identifiers: Canadiana (print) 20260184829 | Canadiana (ebook) 20260187666 | ISBN 978-1-77041-880-6 (softcover) | ISBN 978-1-77852-577-3 (EPUB) | ISBN 978-1-77852-578-0 (PDF) | ISBN 978-1-77041-934-6 (special edition)
Subjects: LCSH: Kreviazuk, Chantal, 1974- | LCSH: Kreviazuk, Chantal, 1974-—Marriage. | LCSH: Maida, Raine. | LCSH: Maida, Raine—Marriage. | LCSH: Singers—Canada—Biography. | LCGFT: Biographies.
Classification: LCC ML400 .K92 2026 | DDC 782.42166092/271—dc23

This book is funded in part by the Government of Canada. *Ce livre est financé en partie par le gouvernement du Canada*. We acknowledge the support of the Canada Council for the Arts. *Nous remercions le Conseil des arts du Canada de son soutien*. We would like to acknowledge the funding support of the Ontario Arts Council (OAC) and the Government of Ontario for their support. We also acknowledge the support of the Government of Ontario through the Ontario Book Publishing Tax Credit, and through Ontario Creates.

Canada

Canada Council for the Arts | Conseil des arts du Canada

Ontario

ONTARIO ARTS COUNCIL
CONSEIL DES ARTS DE L'ONTARIO
an Ontario government agency
un organisme du gouvernement de l'Ontario

ONTARIO CREATES

PRINTED AND BOUND IN CANADA

PRINTING: FRIESENS 5 4 3 2 1

To our three beautiful boys
Rowan, Lucca, and Salvador

☆

Marriage is
about finding each other
over
and over
again.

–Chantal & Raine

PREFACE

THE WITNESS PROTECTION PROGRAM

We've said so little and so much.

Now that I have read this book through again, scanning for grammatical errors and lapses in judgment, I feel there is more to add and subtract, and that I will have regrets. After all, words are like toothpaste, and you cannot put them back in the tube.

That said, I have some gratitude to express for the people who have come to the house Raine and I continue to build and renovate, and this feels like an appropriate time to say thank you.

All the therapy and coaching in the world wouldn't have helped if not for the audience we sing to, and the collective of curious, yearning and open hearts who have shown up for our vulnerability. You, as our witnesses, have allowed us to see ourselves through other, fresh eyes, truly enriching and expanding our perspective of what is fair, dignified, loving behaviour. People often ask us what the secret to our longevity is. September 21, 2026, marks thirty years since we met at Maple Leaf Gardens for a concert we both went to on a whim. On the phone, I told my dear friend Sophie that I have proofed this double memoir for the final time. She said, "And how are you feeling?" I told her that I am letting go and feeling good, but I noticed

Raine writing about how I am hyper-dialled to analyze and dive deep and really immerse myself in coaching and the neuroscience of coupling. I told Sophie that many might say, "Poor Raine. She is too much for him." I look forward to the discussions this book will create, to speaking to the idea of a woman or a partner being "too much." I mentioned that I love the idea of a public forum and getting into such topics with Raine. Sophie sounded wary of that kind of spontaneity. I can understand that. Maybe I'd be putting my husband on the spot—and that's not fair.

Too late. Our show wouldn't be our show without this kind of in-the-moment, sharp, teetering on dangerous dialogue. Sometimes Raine and I are duelling spirits on stage, and perhaps we should have kept our original duo name: Moon Vs Sun. I told Sophie that these "gotcha" moments work because of the audience. This is how we feel safe to speak our mind and even air out grievances in this "witness protection program." We both laughed—it's funny because it's true. This honesty, this incredible willingness to share, isn't lost on me. And it makes for some great entertainment. But Raine's willingness is so courageous, and that speaks to something in me I don't have the words for. There's a quantum physics to it all, in my mind. We change when we're being watched. Our consciousness shifts. We behave. Keep the camera rolling, I say, and let's keep talking about it all, together.

In this ultimate and epic collaboration, we all can grow out of patriarchal roles and the idea that someone is "too much" when they show up with their full and emotive heart. We are, after all, interdependent. On stage, we hear each other's levels and match them to make a balanced mix. Too much of one does not work. But the same is true if the other projects "too little." Your presence in our story is a main character: it pushes us along to be better on this path, to clear the pebbles out of our shoes so that we can walk freely and become exactly who we were meant to become.

CHANTAL

What nobody tells you about a long marriage is that surviving it isn't the achievement. Plenty of people survive. They stay in the same house, share the same last name, show up to the same holidays—and remain fundamentally alone inside a life they built together. That's not something I ever wanted when I whisked Chantal off to Rome and the Sistine Chapel to propose to her. It certainly wasn't something I was going to accept as we grew older together.

The achievement, the thing that took everything I had, was deciding, time and again, to show up. Show up after our Malibu house was stolen by a New York Yankee. Show up when the music business tries to bleed my soul at every turn. Show up when devastating mudslides and fires—disasters that could test any couple's resilience—tested ours. Show up when your partner gets vulnerable and lets you know *we* need help. I sat across from someone that I had hurt—and been hurt by—with a coach who asked questions I didn't want to answer, and chose to be seen anyway. I did the work not because it was easy or comfortable or natural, but because she was worth it. Because *we* were worth it. Because my family was worth it.

I'm Going to Break Your Heart is not supposed to be a perfect love story. It's a rock n roll love story, which means it's bumpy. It has crazy highs and wild lows, and as much as I could never have predicted this when we started our journey, I also feel an obligation to show up for our supporters—those who have lived this journey with us on some level. No matter who you are or where you're from, we all know what it feels like to lose, to laugh until it hurts, to fall in love with a song. These moments belong to us all. They're better when we share them.

RAINE

GETTING HELP

The rental car was quiet. The sun cut through the windows, aggressively lighting portions of Raine's face and abandoning the rest in complete darkness.

We pulled up to a simple wood cabin surrounded by soaring maple trees. The doors of the car shut crisply in the forest stillness. Fatigue made every sound and gesture unbearably significant. From swallowing to shifting in a seat, coughing to unbuckling a seatbelt—everything felt pronounced and deliberate. There was nervousness between us, an awkwardness. The anticipation of the three days ahead made us feel young and new to each other, as we grabbed our two small bags from the trunk.

We weren't meeting Dr. John Grey on the eighth floor of some medical building at Avenue and Eglinton. There was no receptionist telling us, "He shouldn't be much longer." We didn't walk by walls of accreditation, gold-stamped certificates behind glass frames. Instead, we were sent a list of Airbnbs in Sonoma County. We would select our favourite, and he would come to us.

I had found Dr. John after an exhaustive search, asking friends for referrals, scouring the internet for help. I'd brought up the idea of coaching to Raine in bed one morning, casually. He responded with a loving misread: "Sure, babe. We'll get you the help you need."

I remember the couch in the Airbnb's living room. It was dark green, and obviously too soft, the kind of couch a cat might plop on, only expensive. The kind that slowly takes on the shape of its surroundings, like a melting candle or a codependent partner.

We heard a car pull into the driveway, followed by footsteps on the front steps. We stood instinctively, adjusting our posture like kids in a classroom during a surprise visit from the principal.

John walked in carrying all our hopes—and the pieces of a deconstructed chair. He stood in front of us and began assembling it, slowly, meticulously. We waited for what felt like hours, days, a lifetime, until he'd finished. Then he sat down, exhaled, and said, "I'm John. You found the place okay?" He then answered the question our expressions were asking. "Right. The chair. I love this rocking chair. I take it to all my sessions."

It was the perfect introduction to him. A clear indication of how willing he was to be authentic. He was centred and unafraid of judgment, which made him feel instantly trustworthy.

He seemed willing to delay the start of our work, both as an act of mercy and maybe to demonstrate how much control he would have over our lives in the hours to come. The pace was in his hands alone. Like a point guard controlling the tempo of a game, this was John's strategy.

He held us like an uncomfortable silence as both Raine and I began to feel more deeply disarmed. We were equally in the dark, arriving at this moment side by side, not one ahead of the other. I wondered if perhaps even the setting, the shared anticipation and mystery location was part of the therapy. As if John's method began before he even arrived.

His technique felt intentionally disruptive. It wasn't a single hour. It was days—long enough for our rehearsed monologues to run dry, for our private, repeated accusations to dissolve. The structure itself forced prioritization: arranging childcare, calling off work. It demanded seriousness. A session that might normally have happened between errands, in separate cars, was replaced by a unified journey, a flight to Sonoma County, a long drive into the woods, and three days with a man named John.

There was a real cost here. Financial, of course, but also ego—the cost of tearing down the veils we'd built to survive one another. John was trying to return us to who we truly were before the projections and myths. Warts and all.

At my core, I believed John would, well-intentioned or not, blow up my life and marriage. We had three little boys at home, and we really needed to keep this thing together. But just being together wasn't enough for me. I wanted better than together. I wanted to be obsessed with together—the way we were when we first met, and for years after. I couldn't find the moment that feeling changed or where it went. Why didn't it feel like it used to?

Raine had become my subconscious. My person. My foundation. My partner. He was woven into how I function—or don't—as a human being.

Avoidance wasn't our style, and running wasn't an option. So that left this: getting help.

John began simply: "So, how are things going?"

Raine and I each took a swing at answering. Our performative civility quickly unravelled into a pathetic display of infantile tantrums. We got louder and louder, arguing over who was more to blame for the erosion of our marriage. John listened, patient—then he raised his hand and made a gentle signal for us to stop, bringing his thumb to meet his fingers like a bird's beak closing. In another setting, a gesture like that might've felt condescending. But not here. Here it felt like structure. Efficiency. An adult version of a talking stick. An unspoken cue that meant, *your turn is over.*

Once we'd quieted, John turned to Raine.

"Raine, it sounds like Chantal is pretty wound up. She has a lot going on. She's got some history, doesn't she—some tough stuff. What do you think she needs?" Raine took a breath. "Well, I think she needs to maybe get some help."

John nodded, then asked, "Who do you think can help her, Raine?"

I sat silently, feeling exposed. Like I was in a penalty box. Like I was the one who brought us to this stark, unsparing moment in our relationship. There was a pause. Then Raine said, "I don't know . . . her doctor? A therapist? A psychiatrist? You?"

I pictured him relieved. Maybe he thought this was the moment he'd finally get vindication. A professional would confirm his worst fears, *You're right. She is too much. She is the problem.*

Instead, John looked him in the eye and said, "Actually, Raine, do you know who the only person is who can help her?" Long pause. "Who?" Raine asked. "You," replied John. "You're the only one. You're her healer. And she is yours. We were placed on earth to find each other and heal each other's nervous systems."

"THERE IS NO QUICK FIX. IT'S SLOW. THE PACE OF LOVE."

I saw this land on Raine's face as I slowly drifted backward into my life before him. Back to the way frigid cold cuts through bone on a street corner in Winnipeg. The sound of my father's voice. The smell of my mother's cooking. A subtle, constant beep in a hospital room. The smile on Raine's face. The entire life that led me to him, then ultimately to this moment on a sagging couch, in an Airbnb outside San Francisco.

John saw in us the faces of so many couples who had arrived at his doorstep lost and desperate for miracle cures. He looked at us and said, "There is no quick fix. It's slow. The pace of love." Then, quietly, "So, let's dig in."

SEBASTAPOL, SONOMA COUNTY

The idea of love demands safety. Safety to voice your thoughts and feelings. Safety to be vulnerable. Chantal had no problem voicing her feelings. She's as close to an empath as I've ever met, and those deep feelings never excluded our relationship. When she unexpectedly asked me one evening, after making love, if I'd be interested in talking to a marriage coach, I was shocked.

Or was I?

If I'm being honest, I knew there were challenges in our marriage. As artists we spend our bandwidth pouring our hearts out into our music. Writing about our feelings in the lyrics. Mirroring that back to a partner was never something I thought necessary. Whatever you wanted to know was in my songs. Deep down I knew this wasn't good enough. Chantal wanted more connection. She needed me to evolve but not in some glacial one-hour-a-week manner. She wanted it now.

I agreed to see Dr. John Grey, a neuroscientist from Stanford who left to open his own marriage coaching clinic. He was up in Sonoma, and the thought of being in wine country while having to brave the good doctor felt like a good trade-off, so I told Chantal we'd get her the help she needed.

I remember the drive from the San Francisco airport, over the Golden Gate Bridge into Sonoma County like it was yesterday. We hardly spoke. Both trying to figure out what was to come, as I quietly attempted to build a case for my lack of emotional IQ. I knew I was in for revolution. We were heading to a three-day retreat, far from the cliché of a stale therapist office where we'd sit on a couch for sixty minutes every Wednesday at 3 p.m.

We pulled up to a charming little wine country home with a separate one-bedroom unit at the other end of the driveway.

Dr. John greeted us on the gravel driveway and asked us to join him in the main house once we were settled. I unpacked my stuff. Still barely talking, we walked over to the main house. This was to be our home for the next seventy-two hours. My sweaty palms were a dead giveaway that I was nervous. Apprehensive about how much I'd have to confess to.

Turns out it was a lot.

BAND LOOKING FOR SINGER

I'd routinely looked through numerous ads in *Now* magazine and at my local music stores, but this one felt different. *Band looking for singer.*

This particular ad cited Bauhaus, Peter Murphy and Sisters of Mercy as influences. I loved Peter Murphy. I'd bought his "Cuts You Up" single that year at HMV.

Growing up in Toronto, our local alternative station, CFNY, played a lot of British music. I was attracted to and influenced heavily by artists like the Cure, Siouxsie and the Banshees and Joy Division.

In May of 1990, grunge hadn't really hit yet. Most of the scene was still stuck in hair metal: painted nails and tight pants, black makeup, chains, leather cuffs and innumerable other fashion choices that I couldn't imagine myself embracing.

At this point, I had just been kicked out of the prestigious Ridley College in St. Catharines for starting a rock band at school, and sneaking out on weekends to play shows. I refused to cut my hair and started paying less and less attention to anything that wasn't music.

The headmaster, Mr. Packard, called me into his office one rainy spring day. I had never seen the inside of his office, but here I was being asked to take a seat on the tight mahogany leather, Mr. Packard would be with me shortly.

Mr. Packard may as well have had a spotlight shining on him as he strolled in, oozing wisdom in a dark blue suit, with a professor cloak hanging off his back. He greeted me with his deep voice and thanked me for coming by.

I already knew I had overstayed my welcome at the school; I was well aware of my indiscretions, and was purposefully pushing back against certain teachers and the system in general. I prepared myself for the worst, an aggressive lecture seeped in disappointment followed by an abrupt expulsion.

Underneath his headmaster exterior, Mr. Packard revealed a part of himself that I hadn't seen in the four years I'd been at Ridley. He started the conversation by acknowledging my passion for music and how he thought boarding at that school any longer would hold me back. Even if this had been his polite way of expelling me, I was grateful for the heart to heart. We agreed on an arrangement, wherein I would graduate early.

It was surreal to end up at a boarding school in the first place, then just as surreal to find myself back in Toronto now living with my dad. I went to work right away. I needed money for a new guitar and a car to eventually get me to the band rehearsals—which I didn't have yet, but was working hard to find.

Construction was tough, early mornings and hard physical labour. The winter was especially brutal, working outside. The steel in the toes of my work boots would freeze. I'd sit in my Ford Tempo at lunch and during breaks, with the heat blowing full force to try and defrost the steel toe caps. Other than that, I didn't mind the work. The dirt all day was bad for my allergies and asthma, but moving lumber or drywall around and cleaning up basements allowed me time to think and plan. I was planning all day long, writing melodies in my head, lyrics to fit those melodies, melodies to fit lyrics, songs to fit some future band.

Band looking for singer.

I called the number on the ad and spoke with the drummer, Jim. He invited me to audition the following weekend. They were based just outside of Oshawa. I'd never been there, so I left an hour earlier than required. Early and nervous, I knocked on the back door of the house, where I could hear a band playing something I didn't recognize.

I remember walking down a small set of stairs into a basement where I met Mike Turner and the bassist Paul. They were nice, older than me, sweet and inviting. I'd never auditioned for a band before, so I had no idea what to expect. I remembered something I was once told about auditioning: "They want you to get it. They aren't rooting against you; they are rooting for you. You being the right hire means they get to stop looking."

I told them the music I heard through the door sounded incredible. It sounded otherworldly. The guitar was drenched in reverb and delay. It reminded me of the first Cult album and the song "She Sells Sanctuary." The rhythms were atypical and singular.

I asked if that was something they wanted to work on. They loved the idea of working on a new song together. I was thrilled they didn't ask me to begin with a cover song. I never saw myself as someone singing other people's songs. I had too many words and melodies desperate to get out to spend time on music that had already been written.

We worked on that first idea for a while until we homed in on what sounded like a semblance of a song. It was a thrill being able to punch holes in the music, create and shape images I'd only ever conceived in my head.

The entire afternoon was already a bit of a blur, as I hopped in my car and drove back to the city. I knew they had auditioned a bunch of singers before me, and had a few more to get through. I didn't expect them to make a decision in the moment, even though I felt an energy and thought I'd caught glimpses that they felt the same.

The waiting killed me. The experience alone had been profound. It had materialized ideas and visions that I had previously been nurturing alone in my dorm room and on construction sites, in half-finished basements in frozen work boots.

All I wanted was to relive it, to touch that feeling again. The desire was so pure, so in the moment. It had none of the fantasies of future fame. I was addicted to that creative energy. Hearing my words expressed through melodies validated their meaning in ways I hadn't known before. I forced patience believing that *what is truly right for you will be yours.* If this was really right for me, I need only to wait and trust.

A few days later I received the call from Jim, offering me the gig. It wouldn't end up being Our Lady Peace for a good eighteen months, but the journey had officially begun.

“THE JOURNEY HAD OFFICIALLY BEGUN.”

THE GIRL AT THE SHOW

In the fall of 1996, we had just begun recording *Clumsy*, the follow up to our 1994 debut album, *Naveed*, in a studio north of Toronto. *Naveed* had done well, really well, and on the other side of it we had signed to a US record label. Even with our seemingly overnight surge of success, we'd never really entertained going to New York or Los Angeles to record, although it was suddenly an option.

As a new band, you work tirelessly for years to find yourself, share your most authentic voice and then bottle that chemistry for no money. Then, if it works on a large scale, you are encouraged to change the equation you fought so hard to find. The offer to change the recipe is compelling, but conflicts with all the work you've done to get to that moment in the first place.

This always felt clear to me from witnessing other people's success stories, so I was adamant about staying in Toronto to make *Clumsy*. I preferred the beat-down industrial complex that housed this magical little studio owned by our producer at the time, Arnold Lanni. It was the same studio where I did the very first Our Lady Peace demos with guitarist Mike Turner. It wasn't far from where I grew up in the west-end Toronto suburb of Etobicoke, and I loved the neighbourhood familiarity. It felt fitting for an album that circled issues from childhood to be recorded blocks away from the real events. My memories didn't have far to go to find me.

Arnold had cut us a deal early on. We could get a cheap overnight rate at his studio once all the higher-paying artists, funded by big labels with huge recording budgets, had left for the day. We recorded those early demos from midnight to 8 a.m. for a week straight, with nothing but an engineer and as much Tim Hortons coffee as we could afford—which, even with very little money, is quite a lot of coffee.

By 1996, not much had changed since those early demo days, except now we had a budget that allowed us the freedom to go home at midnight. Our success had bought us full-night sleeps and proper meals—lesser celebrated symbols of professional ascension.

We would go to this Italian restaurant named La Fata almost every night, comfort food that we could afford, plus it was only three minutes from the studio. It was family-owned and rustic, with hung bundles of dried garlic and that one huge novelty bottle of wine.

Eventually the owner, Tony, knew us by name and order. I had the same pasta each night: garlic, olive oil and rapini. The meal would undoubtedly end with an espresso, fuel before returning to the studio. Becoming a creature of habit felt essential; like a uniform, it meant energy was never misplaced. The music got every part of me, every part of us.

The *Clumsy* sessions were long and arduous, as we attempted to expand the band's sound as well as our own expectations. The album that follows a hit is hard. It's full of pressure and fear and a desire to evolve without losing the audience you just found. After what seemed to be weeks of straight recording, without a day off, the good people at our record label sent a message through management that Pearl Jam was in town and there was a block of tickets for us. I think they were attempting to give us some reprieve from the studio and each other—a reprieve I never would have offered myself instinctively.

At first, my response to their offer was clear and uncomplicated: "No." Anyone that knew me understood how hyper-focused I was on OLP. It was more than just music. It was my purpose. The songs, the lyrics were proof of life for me, proof of making it on my own.

A voice in my gut whispered, "Go to the show." I tried to quiet it, but as the day wore on, I realized that a night off was probably necessary.

Maple Leaf Gardens was pulsing, the overwhelming energy and anticipation of fifteen thousand people. I walked down the aisle to a block of seats reserved for the band. We'd missed the opener while fighting traffic from the studio, so we found our seats between acts. The house lights were up as the Sony execs mulled about, hand-shaking and shoulder-grabbing.

Company president Rick Camilleri was a couple of rows in front of us. We said hello and I could tell he was happy we made it. I didn't recognize any of the people directly in front of us, but soon after saying hello, he said, "Raine, I wanna introduce you to someone."

As Rick started to say her name, she turned around and in that very moment everything else disappeared. Like a movie or a stroke, my vision tunnelled with only her at the end of it. Staring at me were these crystal blue eyes. She was mysterious looking, multitudinous and unknowable yet classic. She had the most incredible full lips that fought for attention with her eyes, and when she smiled her eyes got bluer somehow, like one charged the other, a surge of electricity. I felt the arena floor move beneath me. She was Chantal Kreviazuk, a new artist signed to Sony. She was my future. Not my future wife, but my future.

> “SHE WAS MY FUTURE. NOT MY FUTURE WIFE, BUT MY FUTURE.”

CLICK

I had every intention of living in Winnipeg forever. There were homes I would drive by in Charleswood and River Heights or the Wolseley area, dreaming that one day I would buy one with my own money, money I would make from my voice and my writing. I wanted to be a fully realized respected adult in my hometown. That was my idea of going places.

I recorded my debut album in Los Angeles with Peter Asher and Matt Wallace after being signed to my first record deal at twenty-one. The studio was in a complex: multiple recording rooms under the same roof, a kitchen or two, a common room and a patio, a basketball net in a parking lot full of men. Men everywhere, all older than me. It was the patriarchy out in full force.

When I arrived, Tom Petty was in the studio up the hall, Keanu Reeves was doing something in the room next to me and Adam Sandler was a few doors down rehearsing for his world tour at the height of his stand-up career. I certainly wasn't in Winnipeg anymore.

The moment I signed my deal, the wheels were set into motion. A whole wave of women were getting their moment at radio, so I imagine this was Sony's incentive behind quickly finishing my music videos and getting my debut album out. Waves come, then just as quickly go. Sony saw an opening and swam for it.

I had never been to Toronto before, and now here I was, shooting my very first music video for my very first single off my very first album. We had spent the previous two days at a number of locations around Toronto. A beautiful girl named Simone would pop into frame between takes to touch up my blush or brush an eyebrow, gloss a lip, minimal touch-ups that allowed me to feel like myself and not an imposter. When someone is spending a lot of time close to your face, it can accelerate the arc of a friendship. Simone had a kind tone and was immaculate at her job, with clean brushes and a gentle touch. I knew right away that she was someone I wanted to be friends with.

At the end of the shoot, we planned a wrap party at the Rivoli on Queen Street, an iconic Toronto landmark that I, as a Winnipegger, had never heard of. Just as we were getting ready to leave, someone on set walked over and passed me an envelope. Simone looked over with interest. As I ripped it open, I saw three sets of tickets to the Pearl Jam concert that evening.

I asked Simone, "Do you know Maple Leaf Gardens very well?" She confidently grabbed the tickets like they were going to evaporate, then flipped through the small stack. "Would you wanna come with me?" I said. She pulled two from the bunch that said "platinum" on them and enthusiastically accepted.

I was fresh as a daisy in the new, cute, tight, vintage Levis I stole from wardrobe, cuddled up to Simone, in the back of the car that took us to the show. It was dark. Entering the venue, I was in front of Simone, but the way I remember it, I can see me coming up the stairs from the view of the seats I was walking toward. My grasp of this moment is like a dream—the kind where your perspective impossibly manages to come from all sides at once. It was as though something phenomenal was happening, and my subconscious was making a note to remember everything from every angle.

It was a sea of seated bodies, no one distinct from anyone else. Then a guy came into focus in the crowd. He stood out like a memory. I could only see the back of his head and a bit of his profile but even still, he was centred. Gorgeous. Calm. Soft. Strong. Wise. Over it. Polite. Polished. Sophisticated. Hunky. Dreamy. I had seen only a sliver of his face and thought, *my husband*, as if we had separated in a grocery store: "You get the milk, I'll grab the bread, then meet up at the till."

"I HAD SEEN ONLY A SLIVER OF HIS FACE AND THOUGHT, MY HUSBAND."

I identified our row and began inching past the line of people who started a chain reaction, pulling their legs into themselves to let us pass—turtle heads pulling into turtle shells. My seat just happened to be directly in front of my nameless husband. I tried to bring my attention back to myself, my row, Simone, Pearl Jam and the president of Sony seated to my right. We chatted for a moment. The room was dark, and a pressurized anticipation vibrated all around. I yelled, "Hey Rick, who is behind me?" He screamed back over the echoing arena chatter, "That'sRainefromOurLadyPeace." I said, "Sorry?" He said, "RainefromOurLadyPeace." Long and bleeding into itself.

Raine's name, even while mixed into one long melting word, managed to jut out like a sliver, unavoidable in a way few words are. It was bold and highlighted, italic, like the only word printed on a single piece of paper. Rick went on to tell me *Our Lady Peace* were signed to Sony too, that they already had a hit album out, *Naveed*, and were in the process of working on their second one.

I hadn't heard *Naveed*, probably because in Winnipeg OLP wasn't yet weaved into the steady stream of Rush and Van Halen on classic rock radio that people from the Peg are expected to blast from their construction vehicles and shops. I found my own diverse range of influences through my cousins and brothers and neighbours, but I hadn't discovered OLP just yet.

Rick then turned me around and said, "This is Chantal, a new signing. Chantal, this is Raine." From this moment on the concert ceased to exist. They could have been shooting giant white Toronto squirrels out of cannons on stage and I wouldn't have noticed.

Raine and I spoke through the rest of the concert. We were in love at first sight, and although we were talking about . . . oh God, who the fuck knows, we were *actually* planning our life together.

He continued, moment after moment, to be everything I saw when I first caught a peek of him. So often a first impression can be misleading, more about you than the actual person, based in projection or a response to a familiar feeling, toxic or otherwise. When it feels like love, it can be short-lived, deflated the moment they talk or breathe or move. The unfortunate tone of a voice can pop a fantasy like an overfilled bike tire. But with Raine everything clicked, and we stuck the landing like Olympic gymnasts. It all just made sense to me. He made sense to me. He was centred. Gorgeous. Calm. Soft. Strong. Wise. Over it. Polite. Polished. Sophisticated. Hunky and dreamy at first sight. Then he opened his mouth, and he was smart. Interesting. Deep. Sincere. He was better than my projection.

I think you can live your whole life in a projection. Almost like a mild simulation you subconsciously create. But at some point, the cat comes out of the bag. The real person is revealed. The goal is to be self-regulated: to avoid projecting anything on anyone—but that's a lofty ask when falling in love. A lifetime with someone guarantees a slow reveal. We get to know ourselves just as much as our partners get to know us.

I invited Raine to the wrap party. He somehow managed to write his phone number down on a receipt and pass it to me. Our hands brushed against each other; a wave of chills, nausea, and an entire lifetime transferred between us in a single touch.

I was certain he wouldn't come to the Rivoli. I imagined he may have made evening plans prior to falling in love with me. He said he still lived at home. I thought nothing of that. We were kids. He was twenty-six and I was twenty-three. I told him that I was staying at the Inn on the Park over by the Sony building.

After Pearl Jam ended, I went backstage but Raine didn't. We had a quick overly casual goodbye, followed by our groups separating like it was no big deal. Raine was wearing his patent blue-leather jacket. It looked so good on him. His dark hair made his ice blue eyes appear nearly alien, magical and otherworldly. He had an angular jaw and strong features, yet he looked quiet, reserved, gentle and even a bit bashful somehow. He was everything all at once. Having fun in the green room was a challenge, preoccupied by the thought of Raine's face, the existence of his name, the possibility of seeing him at the Rivoli.

We were both dating other people at the time, although I didn't know he was seeing someone, and I am not sure I told him I was involved with someone either. I was trying to be a good human. I was absolutely going to honour the relationship I was in, but also I knew it was over the moment I locked eyes with Raine. Everything that had happened before became simply that, what had happened *before*. There was a part of this knowing that felt clean and simple, like, *if I'm Raine's person and Raine is mine then I can't possibly be right for this other guy, and he can't possibly be right for me*. Simple, unemotional truth.

I walked into the Rivoli, scanning the room. I found him sitting at the bar, his back to me, gesturing to the bartender like they were mid-conversation. He had brought his friend from the concert, who left shortly after I arrived, either uninterested in being the obvious third wheel or because Raine deliberately asked him to gracefully depart once I walked in.

> I got to the Rivoli before Chantal did.
> I looked up from my glass, one hand on the
> sticky bar top and found her impossibly blue
> eyes as she walked in.

I had other people to host and greet at the Rivoli. It was my wrap party, after all. I shook hands and rubbed shoulders with the video director and producer and various crew members. My shoes made a noise like Velcro, peeling off the sticky bar floor, as I looked over my shoulder at various points throughout the evening. I was catching glimpses of my future husband sitting on a stool, comfortable and confident on his own, his elbows perched on the bar top, watching me move around the room. Raine was patient and quite fine to entertain himself.

Eventually the obligatory baby-kissing ended, and I could just be beside Raine. I could finally respond to the magnetic pull I had been fighting all night.

We spent the next few hours drinking, playing pool under puddles of harsh overhead lighting, laughing and just existing in the presence of each other until enough smiles and body grazes were strung together to make leaving the only reasonable choice.

I had brought three giant plastic bags filled with the clothes from the video shoot, as well as my own clothes from my Winnipeg closet. I left them in a waiting car for the length of the concert and Rivoli party. As I began walking out to the loitering vehicle, Raine asked if he could drive me home instead. We stopped at the car, took out the bulging bags and told the driver he could go home. We had to walk to where Raine had parked, halfway to Bathurst on Queen.

> Instead of dividing up all the bags between us
> we each took a couple of the small ones then
> instinctively carried the largest one together.
> We each grabbed one of the handles and carried
> the bag the way adults swing small children.
> We were instant partners, instinctively.

Raine drove me to my hotel, and as he pulled in, I remember the feeling of not wanting to say goodbye. Not wanting to leave the car or him, ever.

> When we got to her hotel there was a long pause in my truck. We sat in the driveway, my hands sweating. I didn't want the night to end but at the same time, I didn't feel panicked. I felt quietly comforted by a deep knowing that this night was the first of thousands. We said goodbye and I watched her every step as she went into her hotel.

I got to my room, dropped my bags and laid in bed in the dark and thought, *why am I here? He isn't here. I need to find him.* I was very nervous to call his house. I didn't want to wake his family, and I had a boyfriend I had not yet ended things with.

> My house was dark when I got home so I crawled into my bed with what felt like the most incredible secret. I was exhausted but sleep felt impossible, so I tried to call Chantal. Something in me needed to know she was having the same feelings. I needed to know this chance meeting was having the same effect on Chantal as it was on me. I dialled.

I dialled. I couldn't help it. He was my person. I felt almost lost in my hotel room without him. I needed him to help me find my way home.

> I dialled the hotel only to realize I had no idea how to accurately spell her last name. What I thought I might have heard was wrong and as many times as I tried to spell her name for the front desk, they wouldn't put me through without the correct spelling. Part of me

> conceded, as if the gods were letting me know I needed to slow down a bit. After all, I'd only met this person five hours ago. Moments later my phone rang.

He answered. I was relieved and scared. I told him that I was so sorry for calling him and was it okay, and he said, "Hold on . . ." A blipping dial tone revealed he was jumping over to the other line. I was concerned, but also it was a little exciting. Who was he talking to over there? What was going on at his house? He came back moments later and said,

> "Sorry. That was the receptionist at the hotel. I have been on with them since I got home trying to call you there. They wouldn't put me through to your room because I wasn't spelling your last name correctly."

VULNERABILITY

The night I met Chantal was bittersweet, because in the fall of 1996, the tour schedule did not allot time for magically falling in love with a stranger. Despite our overpowering chemistry, we wouldn't be able to see each other much, if at all, in the coming weeks. We were both either busy in the studio or on the road. Rarely did our schedules or planes or cities overlap.

While we were disappointed, our schedules being packed with such similar things exposed an immediate understanding. What may have felt like an impossible life structure to someone else managed to feel aligned and inspiring to us. We got it. We understood the importance of work, the cross-section of work and identity that comes with so many creative fields.

I can see how vital it was for us to be apart during this initial period of connection. It forced us to get to know each other through telephone lines and cell towers. If I wanted to connect with Chantal, I was going to have to do something I wasn't particularly good at, something I had perhaps never been particularly good at: talking. If I wanted us to stand a chance, I would need to be vulnerable and let her in.

Music was my conduit for expression. It's where I felt safe exposing my innermost feelings, cryptically letting them out into the world. Music was a place to be both vulnerable and internal. Filling hours on a call without the benefit of a shareable product at the end was mind-bending for me.

Early on, Chantal would accuse me of not saying much, and that made me more nervous, but she was incredible at gaining my trust. Being an empath came to her naturally, organically. She was connected and open in a way that didn't seem to terrify her. This gift allowed me to open up more than I ever had with anyone.

One of Our Lady Peace's biggest early breakthroughs came late one night after leaving the studio. We'd just been on a three-week tour with Alanis Morissette. The tour was both an incredible opportunity and a necessary break from the constant eighteen-hour recording sessions. We'd just finished recording the song "Clumsy," so we added it to our set to gauge crowd reaction.

You can love a song, think it could even be a hit, then play it live and have it fall totally flat, limp and motionless at your feet. Then you can play a song about which you have no real sense, a song you like and believe in—but who knows?—and have it set a room on fire. "Clumsy" was the latter.

We returned to the studio re-energized after the tour, knowing we were on the right sonic path. The album was nearly finished. It was back to the late nights in the studio followed by 2 a.m. calls with Chantal.

I arrived home half-asleep late one night. I was exhausted in a way that creates space for vulnerability. It takes energy to have walls up, energy I didn't have. Chantal was on the road touring—hundreds of miles and two time zones away—but it didn't matter. We desperately needed to hear each other's voices before the day ended. I dialled her number as I crawled into my bed. With the phone on my pillow next to my ear, I melted. "I think about you all day. I just want to be in the same place all the time."

The conversation evolved into something unexpectedly personal as we started talking about family, and my dad specifically. It's as if she sensed something delicate there. My father is tough; he's an incredible man, but you have to earn his affection and trust. Growing up, the weekends were when I got him. If we weren't watching old Elvis movies on the couch at home, I was sitting next to him and my brother Danny as we drove through subdivisions in his Cadillac. Frames of houses still weeks from walls, and he'd walk me through it all like it was the most natural classroom in the world. I didn't know then how much I was learning. Looking back now, those slow drives through half-built cul-de-sacs were everything. A quiet man showing his kid, in the only language he had time for, exactly who he was and what he believed in. That a man starting out with nothing can build something. That work is love, even when it keeps you away. The parallels between building a house and building a song have never been lost on me. A strong foundation always matters. The conversation with Chantal exposed a buried fear: *What if I never take the chance to express to him what he means to me?* We didn't talk about feelings in my family. My dad worked a lot, and now that my life had started branching away, I worried he would never know how grateful I was for him, how much he meant to me and how much I loved him.

When we eventually hung up, I had an urgent notion to write these thoughts down. I grabbed my acoustic guitar and the notepad I religiously kept next to my bed and started writing. Words flooded the paper, and chords and melodies followed quickly.

I waited until 7 a.m., then called our engineer, Angelo, to see if he'd meet me at the studio before everyone else showed up. I told him I needed a couple hours to demo this new idea on my own. I arrived around 10 a.m. and got to work. A couple of hours later, the song "4am" was complete. I listened back in the control room, and a nervousness overwhelmed me, a nervousness that wasn't commonplace for me while sharing a new idea. The lyrics were as raw and honest as I'd ever written. They were painfully personal, and I was unsure if I'd be ready to share them with anyone, the band first, the world next. Maybe I'd just send it to my dad and leave it at that.

I realized that the conversation with Chantal and the subsequent musical inspiration had lifted an enormous weight off me. In some ways I had already repaired some of the regret and anxiety surrounding my dad, by simply speaking the words aloud.

THE PROPOSAL

It was June 21, summer solstice. Raine and I were in Rome, staying at the Hassler Hotel at the top of the Spanish Steps. When I think of that morning, I see stairs, stairs leading everywhere and nowhere, up to restaurants, down to ravines, stairs that lead only to more stairs. As we were getting ready to head out for the day, I found Raine in a state. He was stressed, fast, nervous and intense as all hell. This behaviour, and our pending visit to the Vatican, made me think maybe today was the day he was going to propose. I was sure I had detected other clues, like a card-player's tell.

We left the hotel via a dingy mahogany stairwell with dark navy carpets and ancient walls, only to enter out onto the bright white soft stone of the Spanish Steps, looking out over the buildings and the statues below, the bright sun and blank canvas of a day.

We moved stealthily down steps, steps and more steps. Raine had my hand and was pulling me so quickly I thought I might slip. We got in a cab and made our way to the Vatican. It was quiet in the car. He was tense, cold, distant. It looked like we were entering a palatial womb as we arrived. This was the Vatican? It was as though God dropped a religion bomb, and this was the sacred crevice that appeared after the dust settled.

It was a race to the Sistine Chapel. We weren't stopping to look at much. I remembered that Raine's parents were both runners and I thought, *Apple doesn't fall . . .*

At this point I still thought he was going to propose. I pushed my suspicion away, figuring maybe everyone feels like that will happen while in Italy. He was wearing a pair of cargo pants, and I couldn't make out the shape of a ring box, so I let it go and just tried my best to quickly and efficiently enjoy the sights on the running tour.

Raine seemed uninterested in everything. Over it. Been there, done that. It was his first time at the Vatican, at least as an adult, so why wasn't he totally tripping out on the beauty of it all? Maybe the plan was actually to dump me in Italy. That would be a twist. Take me to the most beautiful place in the world to rip my heart out. At this point I had started complaining, wondering why we even came here if he didn't want to enjoy it and wasn't going to propose. "Slow down, Raine!" I finally yelled.

I was actually mad now. I sincerely wanted to be there, to take my time and take it in, to wander through its silent majesty for hours. To explore silently with my beloved. I couldn't believe how incredible it was, and I was now having a properly bad time. Sometimes, a bad time in a beautiful place makes the bad time worse. It hits harder, with further to fall from.

> “SOMETIMES,
> A BAD TIME IN A BEAUTIFUL PLACE
> MAKES THE BAD TIME WORSE.

He grabbed my hand, and we raced down the corridor. Red everywhere. I had pigtails in my hair that day, and I was now in a full trot, the pigtails whipping each side of my neck and ears, loosening as I cantered through the Vatican. I imagined they might need some maintenance when we finally stopped at this beautiful outdoor room called the Octagonal Courtyard. Later I asked him how he even knew of it. He told me he took note of it on the way in. He had been searching manically for the perfect spot.

Once we were in this garden paradise, things calmed. He saw a bench ahead and took me there, more steadily, side by side, not dragging me by the arm. He motioned for me to sit down, then knelt in front of me and said, "Nothing would make me happier than if you would agree to being my wife."

Those words, exactly. He opened an iconic blue velvet Tiffany box. There was a simple solitaire diamond in a simple setting of white gold. It was perfect. I looked up at him, blinded by the white steps and Roman architecture. We smiled at each other as it started to lightly rain, a sun shower cutting through the trees in the garden. It didn't last long, but it was a symbolic gentle freshening of the air, a sprinkle of new beginnings. I said yes, and cried as the panic of the day washed away.

We stood up together and got in a buggy guided by horses, then rode around Rome for a few hours in this timeless bubble, wherein the whole world was an extension of our moment alone. I would only experience this particular brand of frozen time three other times: during childbirth.

We stopped in front of another gorgeous landmark and sat cross-legged on the lawn in front of the Tomb of the Unknown Soldier like young university students who thought they knew everything, though we were ourselves just singer-songwriters high on the love drug, not knowing much of anything at all—except that we were on top of the world.

IT HITS HARDER,
WITH FURTHER TO
FALL FROM."

THE PROPOSAL

Chantal and I had just moved in together. We had suffered through this touring cycle, surviving primarily on long phone calls from random hotel rooms. Once our schedules finally calmed down, we simply wanted to be together every minute, so it seemed natural to live together.

Chantal told me about an old saying her dad used to repeat, "Why buy the cow when you can get the milk for free?" I hated that saying. That wasn't me. In an alternate universe I would have experienced that quote as pressure—pressure to settle down, to hurry. I've never taken well to being forced or told to do something, so this easily could have shut down my desire to commit. This was not the case with Chantal. My intention was always to marry her. I just didn't want to rush us into a marriage before I had a chance to create the most romantic proposal I could.

My family had an awful track record; it wasn't just my parents but my aunts and uncles as well who had yet to outwit divorce. I wasn't prepared with the tools necessary to be the first in my family to maintain a successful marriage. I wanted to and naively believed I could.

Knowing what I know now, I maybe should have received coaching even before proposing—or at least shortly after—but we were kids with such hectic schedules, and I didn't yet have a real sense of how much work it would take to maintain a healthy partnership. I only knew she was it for me. The rest we would figure out together.

> "I DIDN'T YET HAVE A REAL SENSE OF HOW MUCH WORK IT WOULD TAKE TO MAINTAIN A HEALTHY PARTNERSHIP."

☆

That summer, the band had just finished two years of extensive touring—including the arena tour with Alanis, festivals in Germany and France and endless radio festivals in the US—and after some four hundred shows that frantic pace finally came to a halt. We now had a chunk of time blocked off. It was August and this was my perfect window. I would whisk Chantal away to Rome and propose there.

We booked the tickets and hotel. I bought the engagement ring along with two wedding bands. I'd later learn how presumptuous this was: I not only wanted to get engaged but also married in Italy. I had the girl, and I had the plan, all that was left was to roll it out.

The trip's first couple of days were wonderful but a little tense, as I tried to figure out exactly where to propose. We did the tourist thing, ate incredible meals, drank local wines, and finished every evening with the best gelato on the Spanish Steps near our hotel. We walked aimlessly and endlessly around Rome until I decided the Vatican would be the place. We were, of course, going to visit it anyway, and there were so many beautiful gardens and piazzas around there. It would be perfect.

The next morning, I got us up and out of the hotel early. Even at that early hour we fought the Vespa exhaust and August heat. It was tourist season, so the lines were painfully long, packed with every type of tourist you could imagine: screaming children, crying babies, exhausted parents, seniors in love, dogs about to be turned away. I was doing my best to hide the ring in my pocket. I kept it in the box so I could open it in front of Chantal. I don't know why it was so awkward, trying to conceal a velvet cube in a pair of cargo pants. Slowly opening the box in front of her felt like an essential step in a proposal.

The crowds moved slowly through the different Vatican rooms as I dragged Chantal past groups of people studying the massive frescoes and art. I couldn't have cared less, though I tried to appear interested. On the way in we passed a gorgeous outdoor space, the Octagonal Garden. It was full of plants, bougainvillea, Italian cypress trees and stone benches. I had been looking for the perfect spot all day. The moment I saw it, I knew. The problem was that I wasn't sure how to get back to it. The Vatican can be like a maze if you're not careful, especially with such large crowds of people wandering aimlessly. I was sure we were close to the garden, just a few more turns. Before she could stop the holy treasure hunt, the arched entrance appeared in front of us.

We stepped out into the garden where it had begun to rain. I guided her to a stone bench, asked her to sit then got down on one knee. The anticipation of this moment had been building for months, and more intensely since we boarded the plane in Toronto. It was as if I was having an out-of-body experience, a kind of Transcendental Meditation like I wrote about in my song "Starseed." It felt like life imitating art, imitating life.

It was almost as if I was watching myself from above, like a dream, the kind where your perspective impossibly manages to come from all angles at once. My subconscious was making a note to remember everything. I wasn't sure the words would come out, but as I looked up at this absolute princess, her crystal blue eyes and full lips and bright smile, I pulled out the ring and said, "Nothing would make me happier than if you agreed to marry me." Then I thought, *What the fuck! Was that a question?* I knew as it came out that it wasn't exactly what I'd rehearsed. For someone who takes such pride in writing words, this flubbed performance was deeply disappointing.

Of course, she understood and the moment she said yes, the bumbling proposal washed away. We kissed and embraced, and it felt as if the weight of the Colosseum itself had been lifted off my shoulders. Everything slowed down as a peaceful feeling came over me, us. Suddenly, I could appreciate the beauty around us. I could finally take in the sculptures, the history. I could smell the flowers, feel the drops of rain. It was as if her "yes" landed me back in my body, back in the world. We'd transcended the past and all the obstacles that could have kept us apart. We'd beat innumerable invisible obstacles to get to this moment firmly on the ground, together.

I was beyond happy and not interested in fighting the crowds inside, so we left. As we walked back toward our hotel, we came across a beautiful old fountain in a square. We took a break and sat on the fountain steps. Next to us were two young guys who looked American.

We found out they were priests who were visiting the Vatican from their parish in Pennsylvania. Somehow they could tell we were newly engaged, and they wanted to bless us and the ring, so of course we let them.

One of the priests asked if he could offer a piece of advice. Naturally I was prepared to have him read a piece of Scripture, at which I would've done my best to not roll my eyes. Chantal said "yes" and the priest began to recite the letters D Y K H M I L Y. We had no idea what he meant until he began to explain that it was an acronym for "Do you know how much I love you." It was not at all the type of Jesus talk I'd feared and expected.

He said, "Leave it anywhere and everywhere. Perhaps under a pillow, or in a suitcase. They'll find it when the other isn't around, when they don't expect to see it, and it will connect you."

> Raine and I watched as he went on to offer this acronym as something you scribble on a piece of paper every once in a while. You hide it where your partner will find it. It's a simple but

> powerful reminder that you're thinking of them and that you love them.

It took me a minute to wrap my head around a priest in Rome giving us advice as nonreligious as this, but it was brilliant. He knew, in his wisdom, that this simple gesture would move mountains when life got busy and partnership got overlooked. He was right. It wasn't exactly therapy or marriage coaching, but DYKHMILY quickly became our mantra. We continue to use it to this day. We tuck it in a suitcase, under a pillow, anywhere it might catch the other by surprise and serve as a thoughtful and sometimes sexy reminder.

> Sometimes I find it next to my sink when Raine has left town on an early flight. Every time I see it, the world goes quiet for just a moment again, and it brings me right back to the moment we got engaged at the Vatican. It puts me in a state like the moment we birthed a baby. I slip away to another place that is perfect and hopeful, like a white blank canvas, a quiet blazing sun in the perfect cloudless Roman sky.

Game-changing guidance can come from anywhere, even a priest from Philly at a fountain in Rome.

THE ACCIDENT

My first trip to Europe looked very different. I was in a brightly lit, intensive-care wing of a hospital—not the colourful youth hostel or cheap cool boutique hotel I had envisioned when I planned my backpacking trip for my twenty-first birthday. As I began trying to pull out my IV and sit up, I told the attending nurses and doctors that I needed to leave. The doctor came to my side and said, "There is too much blood flowing inside of your body. If you move, you will drown. Just be still now."

If I hadn't been in critical mode—full of regret and sadness and self-pity, desperate to go home, yearning for Canada—I would have enjoyed the poetry in that, to drown in oneself.

Nothing was the same after the accident that broke my femur and landed me in that hospital. My creativity and ambition had an incentive—a sense of urgency, explosiveness. In some ways, it was a necessary tragedy, a kick-start to get me on my way, this universal force like a dad releasing the seat of your bike. You realize you're doing this thing that felt impossible just moments before. You feel this rush of freedom, then inevitably you fall.

> "ARE YOU A PERSON WHO STAYS DOWN OR GETS UP?"

This moment introduces you to yourself as if for the first time. Are you a person who stays down or gets up?

I woke up to a sharp light overhead, the single, harsh light source in an otherwise dark hospital room. Its presence arrived in my awareness like a stab. It cut through time and space, shocking me out of unconsciousness. I didn't have the strength to react, so the pain sat on me with nowhere to go. It couldn't even evolve into a scream or gasp, my voice was lying dead in my throat, limp and disoriented and terrified.

My arm was being sutured. It had been cut to the bone, so there were layers to stitch like a stacking doll being fixed from the smallest doll within to the protective final doll on the outside. I would spend the following month at Florence's orthopaedic hospital, the CTO.

I had initially arrived by ambulance, rolled in by a handsome paramedic. In shock, I fumbled out disoriented words with a shattered jaw, "Am I going to die now?" It's only in hindsight that I can really assess how close I must have been to death. The moment itself and subsequent memories come in bits, disembodied sounds and lights. I remember the experience through a needle-sized peep hole. My body's protective shock system offered me just a tiny look into my reality. My sight dipped in and out; I caught only glimpses of the world, split seconds at a time, like flipping through a flip book too disjointedly to see the animation come to life in your hands.

The surgeon told me I had broken my femur, the biggest bone in my body, and that many die from this so I just needed to sit tight and relax. It's hard to relax with a broken femur, but I tried to surrender to the reality of my life. It felt like a labour of sorts, birthing a new self. All this ferocious pain must be carrying me toward something.

I called my parents. We had been in a regular practice of checking in every few days, so when they got a call from the foremost orthopaedic hospital in Italy, they got on a plane.

My mom was next to me after they put the rod in my leg. The pain took my breath away, this violent exit with no way to accelerate new breath into my lungs. I stared into her eyes and whispered that there was nothing in my future that was worth this pain. There was no wedding, no kids, no career. I could feel her heart beating through her forearm as she peeled my hand off her skin to find a nurse with more pain meds.

The nurses had been injecting shots of morphine into the meaty side on the back of my right thigh, that small area that's not your hip but not your actual butt cheek. My left side was unavailable, as my leg had been in traction for a few weeks prior to the surgery, with an archaic mechanism holding the leg in position.

I was told before the surgery that I would be awake for it and given an epidural. They rolled me on a gurney to a sort of theatre. There were screens on one side of the room. While, they had given me something to curb my consciousness, I still recognized the shape of the tool in use, its similarity to a sledgehammer. It's a recognizably horrifying shape. Afterwards, my mom sat at my bedside as my dad went to the street corner to take pictures of where my accident had happened for insurance purposes.

While he was there, a gentleman asked him why he was taking photos. My dad told him his daughter had been in an accident there a few nights before. The gentleman was plain clothed, but told my dad that he was a police officer and had given the guy a ticket for a burned-out headlight. The officer told the guy, "It's dangerous, walk the bike home." The guy told him he would not walk his bike home, because he lived up in the hills. He grabbed the ticket from the officer and peeled away. Moments later, he hit me at full force. I didn't see him in time to get out of the way because he didn't have a lamp on his bike. I only managed to make out his blurred shape in the darkness in the split second before he shattered my jaw and snapped my femur.

The Italian surgeon told us that he had inserted plates and screws. My nerves were not severed but stretched. He worked around things, to avoid creating further nerve damage. When they eventually took the hardware off my teeth that kept the jaw sewn shut, he did it with a prompt, "One, two, three, take a breath," then ripped out the metal floss. He warned a few times, "We may lose this tooth." Thankfully they all stayed in.

When I returned to Canada and college more than a month later, I was ninety-six pounds. I had been about one hundred and forty pounds when I went to Europe hoping for a fun self-discovery trip. I couldn't walk around campus easily. My new pace made it so difficult to do all the things I had taken for granted, getting in and out of a car and making my way around from one class to another.

I was lucky enough to get assigned an incredible surgeon at Winnipeg's Health Sciences Centre. At one point, I went to see him because my jaw was locking shut. I had a gaping wound in my neck that I had sort of given up on. I was managing it myself, covering it by wrapping my hair around it like a makeshift scarf. I was just trying to move on with my life, so I held in my discomfort and just tried to make peace with my new normal.

But this moment was a breaking point. I couldn't open my mouth more than a few centimetres. With squashed words, squeezed through a locked jaw, I told his secretary, "I think I need to see the doctor." She said, "What is the complaint?" I told her I couldn't open my mouth. She went away, then came back and sent someone outside to tell my mom to go get me an overnight bag, that I was being admitted because an infection was setting into the bone.

In Italy, I had asked my oral surgeon if the hardware he'd put in my mouth would be easy for them to deal with and recognize back in Canada. He laughed, "The hardware we use is universal, made in Germany, no problem." Dr. Ziesmann was now performing an emergency surgery to remove the titanium. He was especially concerned about my chin. Once he got into my face, he discovered that none of his tools worked for the removal of the four plates and sixteen screws in my face. He told my mom it would take an hour or two to dig out the hardware that would by now, these many months later, would be grown over like a neglected park covered with vines and tall grass and mud, like New York City years after an apocalypse.

Five hours later he emerged triumphant. Ziesmann had broken a $1,500 piece of equipment trying to pry the machinery loose. In the end it was the three-dollar screwdriver from a hospital janitor's toolbox, meant to replace radio batteries, that was the right fit for the German screws. He said he had his leg up on my chest and was literally yanking.

After six weeks of healing, Ziesmann passed me a handful of popsicle sticks and demonstrated how to sneak the stick in between my upper and lower teeth and just start jimmying. The centimetre-thick slab of wood felt inconceivably thick, like there was no way it would ever fit in the space between my lips. I would slowly push the popsicle stick between my teeth as instructed, trying to lift the concrete block of my upper jaw away from lava rock that had been melded into the earth. Eventually after seemingly not even budging for days, I began to open my mouth again and now, with the freedom of mobility, I could use my voice.

It's been nearly thirty years since my accident. And if not for some of the physical remnants—the snaking scar I have under my jaw line; the visible spot where my femur busted out of the skin; the scar on my hip where they hammered the rod in; the scars on my arms from an ancient Italian street; the paresthesia; the need to continually rehab my quadricep; my constant battle with atrophy and lower back pain and the sudden intense itch in the spot where I was given all of my morphine needles—I would say that that girl isn't even me. I carry the proof of what she went through, but she feels like someone else.

I remember this constant light on the nurse's desk just down the hall. I watched it, unwavering, showing me what felt like a promise of hope. I was too young to realize the full weight of the bullet I dodged at the time. My obliviousness may have been my greatest asset. Now, when I am feeling down on myself about something, I say to myself, *You got out of that bed. You can get out of anything.*

I was desperate to find joy even in the hospital room and had an undeniable desire to share it with everyone around, nurses and doctors, whomever I could convince that everything was going to be okay. I sang to the nurses, with a clenched jaw, Whitney Houston's "I Will Always Love You." Just a year or so later I would sing it to Raine when we went away for a weekend to Florida, a Raine that didn't yet exist in my life, a Raine that would have lovingly scribbled DYKHMILY onto my cast if he was.

I am still healing from that accident, but Raine's love manages to move in all directions at once, like he has been omnipresent through it all, my witness in reverse. As I revisit my past, I can feel him there beside me in the way he often states that he wishes he was. My representative, my protector, my love.

THE ROMANCE OF PATRIOTISM

It was approximately two hours before I would be singing the anthem for the final game of the 4 Nations Face-Off between the US and Canada. The soundcheck on the ice at TD Garden in Boston had gone well, so I felt ready. I had really wanted to sing at that game because of the excitement I knew my dad would feel. He's such a hockey fan, and I just thought it'd be so fun to go out there and represent my country.

My main concern during the soundcheck was making sure I got the French-language parts right. I had decided to sing a line in French toward the beginning of the song instead of the end because I wanted to be able to say the last part in English, knowing that there would be a global audience, but I very much wanted to make sure that Canada's French culture was included.

I went back to my dressing room. A few minutes went by, then a producer of the pregame show came in with a printed lyric sheet and told me I needed to learn the new lyric change in our national anthem. I asked, "What lyric change?" He replied very matter-of-factly, "Oh, you sang the old lyric." I looked at the words on the page and read the adjustment, *in all of us command.*

I'm sure my subconscious was in a fury as the US president had been poking very publicly and brazenly at Canada, calling us the fifty-first state and saying that our head of state was a governor. Then I had an idea. Once the thought came into my head, that was it. The train had left the station. I had been in conversations via text with my cousin Cor and with my dear friend Amy. Outside of letting those two know that I planned to do a lyric change, I don't think that I ran it by anyone else. I really didn't want anyone to cloud my decision. I knew it was a fierce move, and I was a tad nervous, but I also knew there was no turning back now.

I had one conflicting thought though. Would I be stirring the pot? Sure, maybe publicly, fine, but would I quite literally be causing more problems for the Prime Minister's Office, who was clearly navigating issues with our neighbour to the south?

At that point, there were daily threats of severe tariffs being placed on Canada, and I didn't want to make things more difficult, so I texted our prime minister, a long-time friend. "Are you by chance around?" I asked. Within a few minutes, Justin Trudeau replied to me and said, "Yes, we're here. We're about to watch the game together. We're excited to see you sing the anthem."

I told him my plan, and he said that he would not advise me, but he also informed me that our anthem was not some kind of legal scribe. I was reminded of who we are as a country. That's the essence of Canada right there: If someone were to do something like that—change the lyric to our anthem—they would not be imprisoned. We are *free*, after all.

He told me that over the years, yes, there have been several formal changes to the official anthem, but that from time to time people do informally change it, as is evidenced in the change from "our home and native land" to "on native land" by Jully Black at the 2023 NBA All-Star Game.

I took Justin's words about the anthem's evolution as a signal to go ahead and do what I felt I needed to do, and I went out just thirty-nine minutes later and proceeded to sing our national anthem with my lyric change.

It wasn't easy. I had sung the anthem at many Jets games as a young person, which trained me to focus on my voice only and to block out any of the white noise, as they called it at the Winnipeg Arena during playoff games, but this was still overwhelming.

The crowd was going wild, and I was very emotional. I did get one little word wrong on the French part at the beginning, which I'm still to this day so miffed about, but I became incredibly overwhelmed with emotion and increasingly patriotic as the crowd's roar turned to respect and they started singing loudly along with me through the rest of the anthem.

My body tightened, my heart filled, and it was the most patriotic moment of my life. After I finished singing the anthem with my little lyric change (two words to be exact), seemingly without anyone taking note of it, I went back to my room and kind of collapsed. I began to cry in a way I never had from singing our national anthem. It had been a very charged experience. My friend Amy was now telling me on the phone that she looked on X, and it seemed like nobody noticed. I was a little bit relieved to be honest, but then she said, "Oh, hold on . . ."

Over the next few days, I became swarmed by a stream of people and bots, and I learned all about the evils of the Internet in a very up close and personal way. I believe some people were truly offended by my decision to change the line to, "that only us command." My rendition of the Canadian national anthem in protest to the US president's bullying of our country became a global newsworthy moment. Suddenly my name or reference to the Canadian anthem singer at the 4 Nations Face-Off final was on the front page of nearly every major paper in the world and was trending on X in Canada and in America.

There was a moment right before I walked out to sing the anthem where I felt a palpable yearning for Raine, who was at the Rogers Place arena in

Edmonton and about to perform for 25,000 people. Raine and I talk about absolutely everything. He is my sounding board, especially when it comes to business or anything to do with our life in the music industry.

Even at a great distance, Raine supported me in the most beautiful way imaginable. I don't think I have ever felt so seen and validated by my man. He went out on stage that same night and every night on his entire arena tour and held me up. He celebrated me, and our country uniting. He talked about what I did to his tens of thousands of fans mid-show. He riled up the crowd with patriotism and approval, cheerleading for what I did. He literally championed his woman in the most public way possible, and he just made me feel so loved, partnered and adored.

The first time I got to see him after the 4 Nations Face-Off, I went to his Vancouver show. When I got there, there was a giant line backstage that I had to walk past for the band's meet and greet. As I walked up, he smiled so big. The line of fans who saw him see me then broke out in applause.

I declined interviews with all the news outlets, from CNN to ABC News and even the world's biggest podcast, *MeidasTouch*. I felt I said all that I needed to say. I wanted to just stick my landing, so to speak. I didn't need to keep the moment going forever. Seeing Raine stand up for me is all I could have ever dreamed of.

We all want that unconditional love, to feel like our person would fall on their sword for us, that they would do anything for us. They would literally die for us. There was a constant stream of footage from the fans online after all of the shows on that tour, of Raine talking about me singing that anthem and changing the lyric, and my intention to bring the country together and celebrate our sovereignty, and though the little speech was varied, he ultimately would say the same thing. He would say, "My wife Chantal is a badass boss bitch, and I am proud of her."

I will cherish the memory forever because there is nothing better than feeling loved on that kind of level and our partner displaying such affection and respect without reserve.

PEOPLE CHANGE

I married Raine just as my world began to transform. His arrival in my life came with what felt like a force field. No matter what we faced within our own personal dynamic, we protected each other like lions. Our careers were taking off simultaneously, the doors to our dreams opening in tandem along with all the same external shifts, the sticky transformations in friends and family, the glimmer in the eyes of the people closest to us who suddenly saw us as doors to another world. It felt like we were the only two people in the world who could understand each other with such full complexity as we did.

In February 1996—before there was a Raine, before Toronto, before a music video or a seemingly inconsequential trip to a Pearl Jam concert—a journalist and photographer from the *Winnipeg Free Press* came over to our family home to shoot me for the cover of the entertainment section. I had signed not only a record deal but also a giant publishing deal with Sony.

Growing up in Winnipeg is both the best and worst thing that can happen to a person. Being from a small town meant that any successes or struggles I had were known by the collective. News travels fast when it only has a five-block radius to go.

While Winnipeg is small, it certainly isn't without local heroes, like the Guess Who and Bachman–Turner Overdrive. I always thought television host Monty Hall was the most famous person to emerge from Winnipeg. My childhood pal Bryn was family friends with him. She would mention it from time to time, and it blew me away. That was my biggest brush with fame in my childhood life. There were no real connections to the big time. Although I did hear that Barbra Streisand came through town and worked as a singer or waitress or something at some topless bar. I am not sure if that's been confirmed. Coming from somewhere small and unshowy grounded me in the idea that even the most fabulous stories often began somewhere much less overtly fabulous. It is easier to avoid the effects of stardust when you remember that everyone had to grow up somewhere.

My mother noticed that I had perfect pitch at three years old. We had a piano in the living room, a little upright with a corner of chipped ivory on middle C. I would listen to a song then run to the piano and play it back in a way I find astounding now. I attracted audiences with ease, and felt like I had a superpower.

I would go to the Winnipeg Convention Centre with my dad every year for the weekend home shows where he would set up his stand to promote his store, Krevco Pools. The Moir piano shop would be kitty corner, and I would just sit down and play the beautiful Kaui pianos and draw a crowd almost instantly. I was not yet ten years old, playing everything from Elton John and Billy Joel, Liberace to Hagood Hardy. I loved everything, except maybe country. Sorry, country. I loved hymns, I still do. Gospel, R&B, rock, metal, pop, folk—all of it. I was a master interpreter, a little jukebox.

I wasn't playing at clubs or even loudly pursuing a career at that point. I was just doing a thing that felt natural to me. I was the girl that played every request at the end of the party, entertaining the stragglers who were too hammered to drive home. I would sit with the cute boys and girls and impress them with this thing that I somehow always knew how to do. When I signed a deal with Sony at the age of twenty-one, it took everyone by surprise because my gift had yet to present itself as loudly ambitious.

When I was thirteen, my father went to the guy who made the jingle for his store's commercials and told him I was a good little singer, and that he should meet me. I am sure that Danny was just being polite, but he told my dad to have me call him.

It was in his studio downtown, I found my new favourite place. My dad would drop me off, pass the reins to Danny, who was about fifteen years older than me, and I would spend hours in the studio, singing the jingles he wrote.

He could load up new tracks for harmonies at lightning speed, and I could overdub in record time with my perfect pitch, my weapon for creating the best harmonies and blended unisons. We were like big bro and little sister. We were both Ukrainian, so my dad could speak to him a bit in their mother language, which made him feel even more like family.

As I got increasingly comfortable, I started showing him my own music and we started recording it. After I wrote "Surrounded," I met and got the chance to collaborate with Chris Burke-Gaffney, a local music hero who became a part of the team that was my first management/representation. Danny and Chris then acted as my managers and sent the song to someone they knew at Sony. The A&R person called halfway through the demo. The team at Sony asked if they could come to Winnipeg the next day to meet me and hear all my other songs. That meeting ended with an offer. Within a week of signing, I was being photographed—the little local success story.

> **A STAR IS BORN**
> Virtually unknown singer/songwriter Chantal Kreviazuk
> lands $1-million contract with Sony Music

The photo that accompanied the headline was of me, my arms folded in front of my piano in my family home. I had probably just gotten back from a holiday family vacation, because my skin was the type of tan you just don't get in Winnipeg. My father worked hard and always tried to take us on a trip to "break up the winter." Winnipeg winters begin in October and end in March. You could be gone for all of December and still have three months of it left to face on the other side.

I liked the picture. On it, I am strong and confident but grounded. I am not sexualized or exposed.

I have managed to avoid being overtly sexualized throughout my career, with the exception of a few momentary lapses of judgment. I always say that the piano is my pole. I feel for young women who get into this business and don't play the piano or the guitar. An instrument protects you, or at least it protected me. In some ways it becomes a shared focal point, it's a duo even when you're alone up there, it's your body and your instrument. Without it, there's an instant pressure to dance or move or seduce an audience. The piano quickly became my knight in shining armour, protecting me from the dangers of the stage.

In the article that announced my big deal, Danny Schur, my childhood mentor, acted as my manager and told the journalist that I had signed for a million dollars—a sum quoted in the headline. When I read his words, I felt exposed and embarrassed. Everyone would now think I was a millionaire. I was okay with being acknowledged for having talent, but I was nervous that I would suddenly be perceived as entitled. Dan had pumped up the details of my deal to the interviewer in a way that felt untrue. Unfortunately, that moment created a widening divide in our relationship, as I began to experience warped perceptions in my hometown.

When you reach a certain level of fame people sort of forget that you're a real person, that you still have the same number of nerve endings, the same availability for hurt. The reflection of fame ends up being a chance for them to release something living inside of themselves.

> **"WHEN YOU REACH A CERTAIN LEVEL OF FAME PEOPLE SORT OF FORGET THAT YOU'RE A REAL PERSON."**

People have different responses to this shift in environment. For me, I went inward, I became private. I am incredibly outgoing and love people and camaraderie, so it was hard to watch as some of my outward-facing freeness got curbed out of self-protection. After Danny's conversation with the *Free Press* we lost touch. I ended up recording in LA and moving quickly to Toronto when I met my Raine.

In 2023, Chris Burke-Gaffney called to tell me Danny had died of a brain tumour. I continue to wish I had known he was sick; if only I'd known I would have made efforts to rekindle contact.

With the article out on newsstands all over Winnipeg, it was amazing how quickly I could tell who my forever people were—and who my forever people weren't.

A local musician, who had made some Canadian inroads in the '90s, came up to me at Bar Italia, a well-known restaurant on Corydon Avenue. He sat down at the table next to me and my best friend, Tessa. It felt like the Twilight Zone. I couldn't imagine that he even knew I existed, and yet there he was, at *my* table to talk to *me*.

With big-man-on-campus energy, he leaned over and said, "Hey, I heard about your new big deal with Sony." Prior to this moment, just seeing him at the local mainstay, the Spectrum, was a big deal. Just observing him walk in was enough to quiet a room and speed up a pulse. I can't be sure how I responded to him. I think I was stunned by the attention, the attention that was usually focused on him, now dripping out of him and flopping on my lap like a fish gasping for air. He followed up his opening line with, "Record deals don't get songs on the radio. Just remember that." He dropped his knowledge like a crumpled Coke can out of a truck window, then got up and left the table.

I now know what he meant. It's a lot of work and luck once you get your foot in the door. But the gift of his caution obviously came from somewhere. At this moment, for the first time, he came down from the pedestal I had him on and became just a guy, a guy struggling, a guy who grew up somewhere.

The advice sounded harsh, and I was both thrilled with the attention and insulted by the warning. But I put it in my pocket for later: he wasn't wrong. It took a level of tenacity no one could prepare me for to create an entire life out of one song, one signature, that probably wasn't actually worth the paper it was signed on.

After the article, I suddenly got the respect of this spiritual neighbourhood guru guy. I couldn't really tell you who he was or what he did. He was just sort of a landmark of the community, a small-town mascot of sorts, the likes of which all cities have. When I would later move to Toronto that title was held by an unhoused guy who did laps at Bloor and Bathurst, asking for change like an auctioneer, "Five dollars, five dollars, you got five dollars, ten dollars, I'll take ten, ten dollars."

The neighbourhood guru started coming around me with more regularity. It was not entirely unflattering until the night when Raine came to my condo to visit me for the first time in the Peg, over the holidays before I moved to Toronto. We were cuddled into my cozy living room, watching the snow, drinking tea, when we heard the sounds of a pickup truck running in my driveway for what felt like hours, exhaust pillowing over my windows and the orange lines on the street. I knew the body of the truck was warm, and something intentional seemed to be going on inside it. I could almost make out what the cheap seat covers were made of, brown cloth like it could be made of anything, the hot-dog meat of the fabric world.

The lights lit up the lane and flooded through the blinds, enough to confuse our bodies' time clock. Eventually I heard the mailbox open and the truck drove away. When I was sure the person was gone, I went out to see what was in there. It was a letter of some ten pages. The guy had asked me for money a few days before, money to fund his book and some travels he was hoping to actualize. He thought of himself as a spiritual leader, and he wanted to be funded for travelling and a piece of land and building his *community*. I had offered him a clear and outright "No."

✿

I began reading the letter out loud to Raine, embarrassed, not certain what the guy would say next. I was shaking and my heart was a bit broken. I thought I had gained his respect, but I hadn't. I had become something he felt he could exploit and take advantage of. His words dug into me, "You are the worst kind of person because you come from money and now you have your own money." Raine said, "Wait, who is this guy? Your neighbour? What a creep. K, enough."

There was something in the way Raine just shut down the momentum of my pain like turning off a faucet. He managed to be so much bigger than it. He just refused to give any attention to negative stuff. He refused to get stuck in negativity, while simultaneously validating my experience.

The thing about fame, at any level, is that it does sort of feel like a club. Suddenly you have access to this private society of people who all had to be invited. In one breath you're fifteen years old biking around Charleswood with your best friend, then the next you're at some awards event with Matt Damon, and Brad Pitt just walked by and he was really nice though his breath reeked of cigarette smoke. You and Matt have these meaningful conversations, but then, the next day, he definitely doesn't want to talk to you, and this becomes the first time that you recognize that fame is primarily about optics—one night it can look good for someone of that stature to be chatting with you, and the next it can be the exact opposite.

In some ways, I am grateful that the guru and the musician and my city brought me down to size. The *Free Press* article and the subsequent release of "Surrounded" changed my life. If I was going to become a person in the public eye, I was going to make sure that I did it with grace and integrity. I would not let my fear pour out onto my community like molasses, slow and sludgy and impossible to clean up.

PEOPLE DON'T CHANGE

I've always wanted to believe that people can change. Not just in small, micro ways but deeply and fundamentally. I've told myself countless times, "I'll be different this time." New habits, new discipline, new mindset and for a while, I manage it. But eventually, I find myself circling back to the same versions of me I thought I'd outgrown.

It's a humbling pattern to see. I used to think any failure to change suggested a lack of willpower. My mom quit smoking after twenty years. No patches or nicotine gum. No therapy or hypnosis. She just decided to quit and did. That alone set the bar during my childhood unusually high. This example of extreme willpower happened right in front of my eyes. Over time I've realized something quieter, and maybe more realistic: people don't change as much as they adapt. We can shift behaviours, smooth rough edges and build awareness—but at our core, we tend to remain who we've always been.

I see it as this invisible program running in all of us. Dr. John helped me understand this that first day in Sonoma. This programming is written in childhood, in our early experiences, in the ways we learned to cope with love, fear, rejection and uncertainty. By the time we're adults, that programming gets set like the concrete I'd help pour and smooth out with a two-by-four when I worked construction. It's ingrained and shapes how we respond to almost everything. So, when I hear or read about change, I think what we're really talking about is trying to rewrite some code. And that's not easy work. Especially when those circuits have been wired over decades.

For some people I'm happy they never change. Duncan (OLP) hasn't really changed over the years. He's the same salt of the earth, solid, reliable human I met in high school and started my first band with. It's the reason we didn't audition anyone else when we found ourselves needing a new bass player after *Naveed* came out. Sure, I wish he'd be a little less high strung about being three hours early for flights, bus call and soundchecks but his code was written impeccably well. I'm lucky to be in a band with him. Steve and Jason also. Slight quirks, who doesn't have them, but overall, their code is just solid, and it's helped make OLP's last decade such a fulfilling and inspiring journey. I'm lucky to be in a band with all three of them.

The older I get, the more I think maturity isn't about becoming a whole new person. It's about working with who you are, understanding your flaws, tracing where they come from, and learning how to manage them.

In a strange way, there's something freeing in realizing that our programming is hard to rewrite. Over the years with Chantal and doing the work on our marriage I've had that epiphany. As stubborn as I am and as much as I like to think It's about that same willpower my mom demonstrated when she quit smoking one morning, I know it's about refinement and adding awareness to instinct, compassion to reaction. I've tried to explain this to Chantal a hundred different ways and I know she's hoping for more, but the truth is I'm not looking to escape myself. I just want to learn to navigate my patterns and faults with more grace.

I have a lyric I wrote in one of my journals I haven't found a place for in a song yet. It reads "Change isn't a revolution, it's a conversation."

ORDER OF CANADA

You learn very quickly how political the music business is, especially when it comes to awards season each year. I'd been suspicious of the big awards shows even before I had a record deal. I always found these shows to be obnoxious and demoralizing. I'd never thought art should be competitive, so watching one band or artist win over another never sat well with me.

The irony that both Chantal and I have won our fair share of awards, from the Junos to MuchMusic Awards to a Grammy (Chantal, not me) and a host of other awards, is not lost on us. All those awards sit in a bookcase, cramped together on two shelves in a storage room surrounded by boxes of old merch, hoodies, T-shirts, vinyl and the remnants of an old upright piano shell.

To say they're not on any type of display is an understatement. This isn't some type of rebellious act—we are appreciative, even if our record label paid for us to win or we got those awards by agreeing to perform live on the shows themselves. Yes, that happened.

The reality is it's always been a business, and we're not naive to it. Why we keep those awards hidden probably deserves some therapy. Is it possible to feel shameful for winning an award? If so, that could be the ultimate confirmation of an exhausted Canadian stereotype. But in 2014, Chantal and I were informed that we had received a different type of award.

We both received formal letters, deliveries via courier on the same day, from the Governor General of Canada informing us that we were, jointly, to be appointed to the Order of Canada. This was different. The process for receiving the Order of Canada was nonpartisan and merit-based, meaning Sony Music had no influence on this.

By 2014 my relationship with Sony Music was about as strained as it could get. All the people we knew at the start, from the president down to the assistant, were no longer there, so that label felt foreign to us. It started to dismantle just after *Gravity* in 2002, and by around 2007 we were done. It turns out the Order of Canada wasn't bestowed upon us for any musical merit anyway. Music is what helped introduce us to organizations like War Child and allowed us a platform to advocate for mental health and other initiatives, but our music careers were a very small part of the Order, which was for our work as humanitarians.

This was something I'd never fathomed. As much as I can be a cynic about the pomp and circumstance of awards in general, receiving the Order of Canada brought a real sense of pride. To be honoured among people I grew up admiring—from David Suzuki to Leonard Cohen to Terry Fox—felt surreal. We received our letters while my mom was visiting from Toronto for the US Thanksgiving weekend. She was up in our bedroom and noticed an old Polaroid photo of her and my dad from a wedding they attended, before they were married. It still sits on the mantle next to my bathroom sink. I felt a little awkward that she saw that, and in an attempt to divert the conversation, I blurted out that we were getting the Order and the ceremony was in Ottawa early next year.

Her face radiated with pride and joy. Now that my mom knew, I had to call my dad. He is where I get my "casually unimpressed" attitude. He was congratulatory and excited for sure, but it would take others to validate what an extreme honour this was for him to really get it.

That spring both my parents and their respective partners, along with Chantal's parents, met us in Ottawa as we accepted the Order. It was opulent, lavish, and maybe slightly too grand for my taste, but for once I told myself to enjoy the moment. Chantal looked beautiful and distinguished. She accepted the award in the type of dress she wouldn't typically wear, ultra conservative. I wore a grey suit.

To receive the award was remarkable. To achieve this distinction with your partner was otherworldly. Chantal always mentions in interviews how much she loves our project together, because she finally has a witness. A witness to the great things that happen like a day off in Banff or the Order of Canada, but also to the more trying times. This was the ultimate. Having a witness as we received the highest distinction in Canada made it that much more special.

> “HAVING A WITNESS AS WE RECEIVED THE HIGHEST DISTINCTION IN CANADA MADE IT THAT MUCH MORE SPECIAL.”

When one of us is getting angry at our kids on airplanes or succumbing to road rage with traffic in LA or Toronto, we take the piss out of each other by blurting out “order” beneath our breath, as a reminder to keep it classy.

It usually works.

SURROUNDED

I wrote "Surrounded" while in the shower. I could barely get out quickly enough to find my bulky recorder and tape the idea. It was all there, every word and every melody burst into the universe like the Big Bang or a sneeze. I was in my white towel that had been washed in the soft water system my dad sold at his office, which made towels feel like they were never fully absorbing the water on my soaked body.

I got dressed and ran over to my best friend Tessa Emery's house to show it to her. I played everything for Tessa and her family. I was Chantal the human jukebox, Chantal the artist in residence. I could smoke and drink cans of Coke there, and play video games and dream and talk philosophy and there was no religion. I was free to be whatever I was there. I loved her family as much as my own. They had their own shit, of course, but somehow when I went over to her house, my shit and their shit simultaneously stopped and there was peace.

Mrs. Emery would always chime in about my songs. I felt like she was perhaps more honest than my parents, who loved everything I sang and wrote. Mrs. Emery poked holes, asked questions, picked favourites, so if she loved something I knew it must be good. She was a tough customer, and therefore the most important to impress.

Tessa and Mrs. Emery sat intently listening, their eyes closed, taking in the lyrics and melodies of "Surrounded."

A year beforehand, close family friend Samuel died by suicide. He was so handsome, and his laugh and personality were so infectious. He was athletic but with the perfect Winnipeg blend of cool, hippie and jaded, though he was a dentist's son and from the rich part of town, which conflicted with his whole non-corporate vibe. His mom was this awesome boho lady I continue to adore. She had this store in Osborne where she sold beautiful things she found in her travels to places like Morocco and Thailand. She had five kids, and four were boys. She had my dream family, and she had Samuel.

The night he died, I was waitressing and called home to ask my parents if I could keep the car a little longer and hang out with some friends from work. I was the type of daughter I'd be terrified to have. I never came home when I was supposed to. My dad picked up the phone and said simply, "Come home." He had to talk to me. I heard my mom in the background tell him not to tell me on the phone, and then I demanded he tell me what was going on. He said, "Well, we think Samuel is dead. It sounds like he took his life."

When I got home, my dad took me to Bryn's house. Her family lived on Park Boulevard in a big old beautiful stone house right behind Samuel's place on Lamont, in the Old Tuxedo neighbourhood right along Assiniboine Park.

We were like a congregation at Bryn's house as we sat there waiting for some kind of news. What possible news could there be? He was gone. You can't know that you don't have tools for a moment

"YOU CAN'T KNOW THAT YOU DON'T HAVE TOOLS FOR A MOMENT LIKE THIS, UNTIL THE MOMENT YOU DESPERATELY NEED THEM."

like this, until the moment you desperately need them. A parent asked me to go to the other room. Someone didn't like that I was there, or that I was as hysterical as I was, or that I had told them they should have reached out to Samuel more. Like maybe they could have done something to save him. Now, I can imagine few more unbearable things than your son's teenage crush doling out blame.

My dad took me to the funeral. It felt so odd, going to a place where Samuel was, but of course wasn't. I knew he was just lying there in the white box, so close but so far away. There were so many people at his funeral, this community that loved him.

I know he didn't love me like I loved him, but he held my hand once as we walked down Park Boulevard in broad daylight, and it made my teenage life worth living. Samuel didn't just hold anyone's hand. He was *the* guy. He played hockey and loved Bob Marley. He showed me Spirit of the West, and I showed him Yes.

When I wrote "Surrounded," everything changed. Not just because it was the catalyst for my career taking off, but because somehow it made me feel hope. Even after he was gone, he continued bringing me to life.

One night before he died, he quite nonchalantly said that he knew I would make it. He said it as if it had already happened. It was like he really knew. He saw my talent, maybe into my soul, and knew my potential. In moments when I find myself trying to make peace with his death, I circle back to this moment and this otherworldly quality he had.

I was depressed while recording my album, because I thought the demo of "Surrounded" was so good. In the music industry, we call this, demo-itis. When you manage to capture something unmatchable in the demo, it becomes near impossible to accept any future iterations.

I couldn't get my head around the album version. In hindsight, the demo was actually terrible. I honestly don't even know how Mike heard any talent in me when he got that version of it at Sony in Toronto. God bless him for hearing *something*.

I still love playing "Surrounded." It connects me to a soul lost. It pays homage to a person who inspired my creativity, and in turn brings to life a path I never could have imagined.

If I hadn't known Samuel or written "Surrounded," I wouldn't have the life I have—including my husband and my children. Samuel's existence became a door to a world. I wouldn't have the opportunities I do to make a meaningful impact on the things I find important. He is a tragic and undeniable part of my origin story.

MOVING AND STILL

The process of writing my second album was filled with a new level of pressure. It was very important to me to write an epic record to follow up the success and reception of *Under These Rocks and Stones,* but I needed to do it while maintaining my authenticity. Nothing is scarier than following up a hit.

I rented a cabin in Uxbridge, Ontario, just north of Toronto, months before we moved to LA in the dead of winter. There, I felt the pain of the world. There was an upright piano in the living room, and out the window to my right there was endless snow. It was like being back in Manitoba. I wrote a song about a girl I'd learned about from a documentary. Her name was Eve, she was from Australia and had died of AIDS. Her and her mother's stories were so compelling and touching. Raine and I had watched it on the couch in our little Toronto condo. The song poured out of me, and it remains one of my favourites to sing in every context, with a symphony or alone at the piano.

I also wrote the song "Blue" at the Uxbridge cabin. It's multitudinous, both soft and compassionate while saying that we're all a bit full of crap, that we're selfish and could be doing more. It's fun to look back at music and listen like an audience, with the gift of time and distance. It's interesting to notice your own habits and patterns. In hindsight, "Blue" sounds a bit like "Before You" and "M" and "Far Away," which I wrote about the passing of my cousin.

While I was happy and proud, I've always felt conflicted about winning best pop album at the Junos that year. I had been up against Alanis and Céline and Joni: the holy trinity of one-name icons. It's confusing to beat actual living legends. The imposter syndrome pops in with lots to say.

I had dined with Joni and Peter Asher and his wife, Wendy, not long before, and of course, fell absolutely in love with Joni. She smoked through the whole dinner like one of her self-portraits come to life. I kept asking her what else I could get for her, just desperate to serve her.

After the Junos, I had a quiet but increasingly nagging feeling that a move to LA might be approaching.

About a year later we were in our Toronto apartment and *This Hour Has 22 Minutes* was on the TV. We were tuned in partially while puttering around our home when I heard my name. The host was making fun of me. He rambled on about me like I was a has-been, over the hill, like everything good that would ever happen for me professionally was in the past. As if to say that I had done nothing since the award. There's a part of being bullied on air that makes a person feel like they've made it, and then there's a part that just kind of hurts. This moment was the final push to move to Los Angeles. It propelled the desire to escape my former self and just be a young woman with her hubby on a beach somewhere.

It has continued to be a mindfuck to know I have a bit of fame. Sometimes I'll walk into a store and the cashier is almost a bit rude. Then I put my credit card down with my name on it, so they ask, "Oh, are you related to the singer Chantal Kreviazuk?" I say, "I am Chantal Kreviazuk."

Sometimes people are in a bad mood, or they don't seem very kind—and then they realize it's me and they light up. I offer something only subtly passive aggressive like, "I'm so happy to see that you're happy now. I thought maybe you were a little down when I first came into the store." To see someone joyfully come to life only after clocking my name can make it a challenge to trust the authenticity of that joy.

I love making new friends, though sometimes when I do, I end up regretting it. Something comes up, a weird ask, a little favour. Just recently a new friend was saying that they were having a Christmas party, and by the end of the evening the last text said something like, "Wow, it would sure be amazing if you would video a message to my fifty-five guests saying happy holidays and maybe sing a little bit of a Christmas carol for a moment." A motive revealed. It hurts while simultaneously not hurting at all. With fame you can be both flattered and insulted, grateful and disoriented.

"WITH FAME YOU CAN BE BOTH FLATTERED AND INSULTED, GRATEFUL AND DISORIENTED."

ON THE RUN

My first solo record, *The Hunters Lullaby*, starts with a song about moving to California, titled "Careful What You Wish For."

The opening line is, "Oh no Ma look what I've done / I'm on the run / I've gone to California." Thinking back on when we decided to move, that line makes perfect sense, because we were running away. Running away from ourselves, running from the versions of ourselves that we'd become. Running from our success.

Chantal and I had it all in 2000. We'd just gotten married at the most picturesque location in Toronto, in a beautiful winter wedding with a roaring fire and quartet, surrounded by our friends and family. We were living right downtown in an amazing loft in the hippest neighbourhood on Claremont Street. We were just a short stroll to Trinity Bellwoods Park, and the first Terroni restaurant had just opened next door. We were surrounded by incredible bakeries and shops and restaurants, and our careers were thriving.

Yet with all of this, we were still itching to leave. I think it had a lot to do with the fact that we've never been fully comfortable being in the spotlight. We've never been comfortable having our personal space invaded.

I have some peers who enjoy the celebrity part of it. I despise it. I don't enjoy talking about myself. I'm happy to let the music do the talking. The irony was that the music started to be harder to make in Toronto. I don't believe in writers' block, but I do believe that forcing music is the death of an artist—and I was there.

> “I WAS LOOKING FOR NEW MEANING THROUGH UNCERTAINTY.”

I needed a Jack Kerouac–style change. I needed unpredictability. I was looking for new meaning through uncertainty. Leaving Toronto, OLP and everything that made me comfortable was at stake.

The simple thought of leaving where I'd spent my entire life was energizing. Unexpected destinations and outcomes would save me.

It's fascinating to think that Toronto could feel small, but it wasn't just the city. We had just finished our fourth album, *Spiritual Machines*, with our longtime producer Arnold Lanni. As much as I loved Arnold, most creative relationships have a shelf life, and ours had come due during the making of that album.

We went down to Atlanta for a couple weeks to mix the album with Brendan O'Brien. That trip was validation that change was necessary, at least on the OLP front. Brendan produced some of the greatest rock albums of the '90s, including Pearl Jam, Stone Temple Pilots, Rage Against the Machine and the Black Crowes. Hearing his stories about how those albums were recorded got my wheels spinning.

I felt like going as far away as I could without actually leaving the continent was going to be healthy. I found it easy to romanticize travelling across the country, heading for the West Coast to move into a little

A-frame in Malibu. Though not the Malibu that everybody thinks of when they think of Malibu. Granted, it was across from Neptune's Net, which is a restaurant that's been shown in a bunch of movies—most famously *The Fast and the Furious*—but we were on a small beach with a cool surf break.

Our neighbourhood seemed to empty out during the week. For our neighbours, it was a weekend getaway rather than a main residence, so during the week it was just Chantal and I, secluded.

We brought whatever we could fit in our 2000 GMC XL Yukon—including, of course, a couple acoustic guitars and a large keyboard, which left very little room for anything else. We didn't ship anything, either. I've always wanted to be a minimalist. I've never been able to get there, but the idea of leaving everything behind and just taking the absolute necessities is a dream.

In a way this was a rebirth. We were starting down a new path together for the first time, because everything up to then had been me absorbing Chantal into my Toronto world. It was true change and independence. As a newly married couple, conscious or not, it felt like that was necessary for our relationship. It was the two of us against the world, which was very different from in Toronto, where there were all these outside forces pulling me, especially, but also pulling Chantal back to Winnipeg.

Before we made the move, OLP was on tour with Candlebox and Sponge. We were coming down the coast from San Francisco and going to LA. OLP had a day off in LA, so I took a taxi up to see the little beachside A-frame. I didn't know just how far Malibu stretches. It's thirty miles long and we were at literally the thirtieth mile, right at the surf break county line. When the wind blew, you felt it go right through the whole house. It was exactly the type of beaten down place I had hoped for. It was perfect for our goal of simplicity and minimalism.

THE RAMONES

Most people will tell you that it takes a highly ambitious, slightly delusional, almost crazy person to make it in the music business. It's a cutthroat industry that the meek rarely survive. The earth is littered with extremely talented artists eaten up and taken advantage of by a music business that is downright criminal and cruel.

I knew Katy Perry was built for this business the day I met her. She came to our studio one day to write with Chantal. As soon as she walked in, she let Chantal know that earlier that day she'd been dropped by her publisher. Anybody else might have cancelled the session and drowned that news in a forty of vodka, but Katy was unfazed. Moments like these were validating. I've always been inspired by people who have the rare type of thick skin and grit that you need to make it in music, who are as relentless as I am, at least in the pursuit of art.

Early on in my career, I saw glimpses of this trait in different artists. On some it reflected an inspirational unwillingness to fail, and in others it cemented the idea of "never meet your heroes."

An exception to that rule was Robert Plant. OLP opened for Page and Plant in America after Robert heard "Starseed" in his limousine while driving around NYC and immediately called his manager to get us on his tour with Jimmy Page. Meeting Robert Plant was surreal, but he was normal. Complimentary about our sound, he recited actual lyrics from *Naveed* to me that he said he admired. He was the rare exception from all the megalomaniacs running around the entertainment world.

Not long before opening for Page and Plant, OLP was asked to support the Ramones. It seemed every call we got at this time in our career was exciting news. It was either "Starseed" had jumped a few more spots on the Billboard charts or KROQ, the leading alternative station in the US, was playing "Starseed"—or that another great band wanted us to come on tour with them.

This was a moment. The Ramones were OGs. A quintessential punk band—although I would be lying if I told you they were a big influence on me, they were nonetheless important. More than their sound, I admired their attitude. I looked up to the Ramones the same way I revered the Clash. These bands didn't give a fuck. Never followed trends. Forged their own sound. They were artists, not businessmen. Like, *screw the man*. Or so I thought.

As our van pulled up to the beautiful old theatre in Poughkeepsie, New York, I remember the twinge in my belly. Never in my life did I imagine OLP supporting the Ramones. We'd played CBGB a couple months earlier. Simply playing at the same venue where bands like the Ramones, Blondie and Talking Heads cut their teeth was a thrill and an honour.

Like every band before us there, we learned you put your jackets in your guitar cases and close them up tight while you were sound checking—not to avoid them being stolen, but to keep the cockroaches from getting in your pockets. CBGB was a glorious rock-n-roll rite of passage, and that's as close to the Ramones as I figured we'd ever get.

Opening for them was next level. The irony is that I barely remember the show. I know enough to remember the audience was mildly interested in us. OLP could've played one of its best shows, but that crowd was there to see the Ramones. We were a minor nuisance, and that was fine with me.

Although I never actually officially met Joey or any of the other Ramones, my experience was memorable. After our show we headed back to our dressing room. It was up an old set of stairs that felt more like a fire escape than a proper staircase, and around a corner away from the main backstage area.

As I approached the bottom of the staircase, I could hear someone yelling. I could make out this heavy New York accent berating someone about—T-shirts? As I turned the corner, I found myself standing in front of an awkwardly lanky Joey Ramone, dressed in all black, with manager Danny Fields. Joey was laying into Danny about not seeing enough Ramones T-shirts in the audience. I remember looking out during our set, and feeling like all I saw was that classic Ramones logo emblazoned across the chest of every fan in the building—but I guess it wasn't enough for Joey.

Now I've never been so naive to not understand that side of the business, but, if I'm being honest, seeing Joey Ramone care that much about shilling more merch hurt a little.

Not long after that Ramones show CBGB turned into a fancy John Varvatos clothing store—a reminder that nothing is sacred.

VAN HALEN

When I was fourteen, my cousin Nick took me to my first proper rock concert. He was like my older brother, and we spent a lot of time together growing up so it was perfect that this rite of passage was going to be shared with him. Like most teenagers that summer, I played Van Halen's *1984* album on repeat. We took the subway downtown, got off at the College Street station and walked over to Maple Leaf Gardens amongst the swarm of Van Halen fans.

I can still remember that distinctive smell of weed when we entered the arena. Different from what you smell today. This was that old rock-n-roll weed. Much dirtier and smoky; you could hardly see the stage through the haze. It was exhilarating. At fourteen, I knew how much I loved music, but hadn't visualized it as an actual career.

The concert was incredible, but it served a unique purpose for me. David Lee Roth was a true entertainer, blending martial arts moves and knives into the show, while Eddie demonstrated what a true master of his instrument he was.

That I would find myself opening for Van Halen on their *Balance* tour across America for an entire summer playing fifty-five sold-out shows is something my brother Dan and I still laugh about today.

The Van Halen that OLP toured with during the summer of '95, however, was not the David Lee Roth version, it was the Sammy Hagar version. It could have just as easily been the David Lee Roth version and the experience would have been just as bittersweet.

We were just starting to break in America in 1995. Our first album, *Naveed*, and the single "Starseed" were everywhere. When the call came in that we'd been offered the Van Halen tour, we had just started a club tour with Detroit band Sponge and Boston-based band Letters to Cleo, in front of two thousand post-grunge kids stage-diving, wearing our merch and singing along each night. It was hot and sweaty and exactly where we were supposed to be. Until it wasn't.

Our manager, Eric, called to tell me that we were going to have to leave this club tour to join Van Halen. I turned him down. He called back a couple hours after we had got off stage in Cincinnati, letting me know that we might need to reconsider. I didn't care. Well, I did care. I was actually sad that I felt the need to say no, but I knew that was the right decision deep in my bones.

We were building something special. Those club shows were electric. It was tangible. This is what it felt like for a rock band to pay their dues, build a career. My appeal lasted until morning, when he called me for a third time and informed me that our US label at the time, Relativity Records, said they were going to drop us if we didn't take the tour.

This was Spinal Tap in real time, threatened by the president of our label, who only weeks before in New York was fawning over us, taking us out for dinner, buying us drinks, planning the future. This wasn't the existential crisis I initially formulated in my head. It was what I'd always expected—I just hadn't expected it to rear its ugly head so soon. The music business was ruthless.

Being played in the same hour between Incubus and the Deftones across American alt-rock radio stations was something we had worked hard for. I was terrified this tour would dismantle that. Make us uncool.

Our agent at the time at ICM flew out to one of the first shows, and let me know over a private dinner that Alice in Chains had the exact same feelings before they accepted a Van Halen tour a couple years earlier. He also mentioned how they admitted it had made them a much better band by the end of the tour. He said Layne Staley learned how to win over fans who had no interest in their set.

This was good to hear, because I had fans in the front rows holding up the bird to me for our entire set. Just as I had started to settle in and accept this fate for the next three months, our tour manager Kevin Meikle came up to me shortly after our set in Minneapolis to let us know he'd just overheard Sammy Hagar screaming at their tour manager, saying that he'd had enough, Our Lady Peace was off the tour.

> "I'VE NEVER VIEWED PERFORMING AS A PARTY, BUT AS ESCAPISM THAT COULD BE COMMUNAL."

Did Sammy figure out I was a fan of the OG Van Halen, and not of this new version? He'd mentioned something to me in passing one day about trying to get the crowd more pumped up during our set. I kind of laughed it off, telling him I'm not that kind of singer. I wasn't. I was being genuine. I was extremely introverted back then, and only slightly better now. I've never viewed performing as a party, but as escapism that could be communal. Sammy was a party. We quickly learned that it was my lack of hypeman prowess that was our demise.

I was shocked. What would I tell my mom? We were sure to be dropped by our label now. Before I could even get our manager on the phone, the Van Halen tour manager knocked on our dressing room. He said the Van

Halen brothers, Eddie and Alex, wanted to see me in their dressing room. My head was spinning as I was escorted to their room.

Part of me felt like I was not only letting my band down, but the Van Halen brothers as well, so my nerves were wrecked by the time we got to their dressing-room door. Walking in, I was immediately hit with the pungent smell of garlic. Alex had a herniated disc in his neck, and his doctor had him wear a neck brace coated in garlic during the day. We had bonded over the fact that I also had herniated discs in my back. Alex was so generous with advice and sharing his doctor's contact. I struggled a lot with my condition on the road, even though I never went full anti-vampire with the garlic.

Before I could say anything, Eddie told me immediately not to pay attention to Sammy and that he had no right to kick us off the tour. We were good.

My shoulders lifted and my entire chest fell, as a long breath left my body, carrying with it all that pressure and stress of letting so many people down. We did become a better band. I learned how to engage an audience better. Not as much as Sammy wanted, but definitely out of my comfort zone.

I've never forgotten how appreciative I was for the Van Halen brothers to stick up for me that day in Minneapolis. I was sad when Eddie passed a few years ago. He was a master. It was rare to ever see him without his guitar on. Alex was his equal on drums—underrated, in my opinion. I loved watching him play each night. I ran into Alex years later at a Black Sabbath show at the Hollywood Bowl. We were all backstage and I went to say hello. First thing he asked was how my back was. He's a real one.

LEAVING ON A JET PLANE

After my first album came out, I left my little twin bed in my parents' house and spent months travelling all over Europe, Japan, Canada and the States while Raine was opening for the Ramones. I had met all the key Sony staff and CEOs from all the territories, and I was exhausted. I had hemorrhoids from stress and a rare, burning tongue disorder that popped up when I was overwhelmed, which for a period there, was 24/7. It was too much, too quickly. In what felt like a matter of days, I had gone from sleeping in like other lost teens to being this full adult woman with a love living a province away and a demanding travel and work schedule all entirely out of my control.

Finally, after months of touring, I had a moment to be home. While during most of my downtime I was desperate to go directly to Toronto to be with Raine, this time for whatever reason I was desperate to be home, back in my childhood bedroom with the smell of borscht wafting down the hall from the kitchen. The plan was to nap and eat and do nothing. Then the phone rang. It was the New York office. They told me to go to the airport, buy a ticket and fly in to cover a John Denver song for a Jerry Bruckheimer blockbuster.

I didn't know who Jerry Bruckheimer was. I didn't know what a blockbuster was, either. Additionally, I had never had sushi, avocado, or artichokes. I was still a small-town girl. I thought yoga and meditation were silly because like, *don't they know we're already breathing*?

When the phone rings and tells you to come to NYC, you go. I was really hoping I would get to cover "Annie's Song," the John Denver song I knew by its opening line, "You fill up my senses." We used to sing that one on the school bus. The hot girl in my high school, Geils Andison, loved John Denver and had some sort of music-playing device. She was the beautiful, rich, blond high schooler on the bus. Geils was like Goldilocks, with a permanent retainer on her bottom teeth, which I found unbearably compelling. I was at an age when confidence plus something a bit different made you the absolute coolest: a cast, a retainer, fainting in assemblies—so cool.

Later some people would say I looked like her little sister, Darlene. I thought that was amazing, because she was incredible and had a huge, beautiful mouth and smiled like Carly Simon. Their brother James seemed like the catch of the century to me, untouchably gorgeous. He paid attention to me once when his folks were out of town, "Sweet Jane" playing in the background. I called his house one night to tell him I liked him. He never called me back.

When I got to New York, it wasn't "Annie's Song" that I was to cover. It was "Leaving on a Jet Plane." I was a little disappointed because I thought that that particular song sounded like a campfire song, a bit hokey with possible smores nearby.

Throughout the process of producing the song—which of course I was not given credit for—I knew it needed to be unique and special, sexy and rhythmic. I had recently fallen absolutely in love with hip-hop music; when Aerosmith's Steven Tyler came out and sang with Run-D.M.C. on David Letterman I knew the world was different. I wanted that feel in my music. If I could have told my younger self that I would go on to have songs with Drake and Kendrick Lamar, I am sure I wouldn't have believed it.

Collaboration can be something of a runaway train. Every project is so different: there is hierarchy and submission, and rarely is everyone honoured and included in the very final product. I don't regret the music I have made. I regret the systems we live in, however. I think that "Jet Plane" is a perfect song because I am so proud of its influences, the purity with which I performed it, the joy and hope I felt at the time. I was just a girl finding herself on a multi-million-selling soundtrack, alongside her boyfriend's band and Aerosmith.

> "COLLABORATION CAN BE SOMETHING OF A RUNAWAY TRAIN."

AMERICAN IDOL

Writing songs is the most personal and vulnerable thing I do. I engage and analyze my feelings through writing music. It can take months to put together an album. You spend all this time writing in the privacy of your own space and head, and then you get out on tour and there you are facing this room of people singing your quietly written words back to you. Touring fills a tank that nothing else does in quite the same way. There is an unbelievable, out-of-body high.

As a semi-introvert, I always found listening more cathartic than talking, and writing more cathartic than anything. Reading back my own words and then singing them continues to be the ultimate mirror for me.

The intimacy of the songwriting process can, at times, make co-writing tough. It's challenging to share this precious space with someone. I need to feel a strong sense of trust and mutual respect to be able to sit down, open up and write with another person. I never looked at writing as a business early on. I had a publishing deal with Sony, along with my record deal, and was well aware that as a songwriter I'd make money if any of my compositions got on the radio or were played on MTV or MuchMusic, but it wasn't until after I'd signed that I learned just how pervasive songwriting is.

I started checking credits, discovering that Prince wrote "Nothing Compares 2 U," which was Sinéad O'Connor's biggest hit, and David Bowie wrote "All the Young Dudes" for Mott the Hoople. This moment revealed this songwriting underbelly I didn't know about previously. It also revealed an opportunity to build out the part of my and Chantal's career that didn't need to depend on a tour. Touring fills a tank, yes. But it also empties a tank that can be very hard to fill back up.

I was a big fan of Chantal's writing. I considered it a privilege to sit back and watch her write her albums back in the Toronto loft when we first got together. I was floored by songs like "How Does It Feel," cowritten with Avril Lavigne, and, more recently, "Unforgivable." Chantal always made it look so easy. These songs would pour out of her in a moment, and before you knew it the song was complete. She wrote some of my favourite songs—by any artist—and she also happened to be my wife.

In 2000 when we decided to move to Los Angeles, a part of the plan was to write together for film. A couple of years earlier, Chantal and OLP had songs on the iconic *Armageddon* soundtrack, and then in 1999 we'd been commissioned by Turner Classic Movies to score the 1917 version of *Cleopatra*, originally a silent film; TCM wanted music put to classics like these so they could air them on their channel. It felt like a window of opportunity: we hoped we could leverage these two jobs into other scoring work.

Not only did *Cleopatra* give us a chance to work together on something creative, but it came at a time when we were looking for a change, a new adventure. I was working on *Spiritual Machines* with OLP and my frustration mostly had to do with the typical album cycle dictated by a major label. At that point, albums were released every two to three years. Big marketing campaigns and touring schedules were built around them. I'd always fought the concept of only having ten or twelve songs released every few years. I wrote almost every day, and I was never comfortable being told what made it to an album. A painter or poet was never constrained by those same parameters. I imagined they could binge paint for two months, have an art show and then do it again a few months later with a new collection. The music business felt broken in that sense.

When we decided to relocate to LA, I remember specifically telling my mom and the devastated look on her face. I was afraid of abandoning her. She hadn't remarried, and we were very close. Even though I hadn't been home much because of OLP, I was worried that our family, dysfunctional as it was, would become more fractured. The prospect of Sunday night dinners, birthdays, anniversaries and holidays suddenly not being a part of my life was unnerving, but the creative need overpowered those doubts.

To soften the blow of a transition of that size, we brought our two dear friends, Sam Nutt and Eric Hoskins, on the trek with us. Together, we'd survived driving all over Iraq and the Middle East on our first trip working with War Child a couple years earlier, so a fifty-hour drive in a cramped SUV would be a piece of cake.

Exactly a week later we pulled into Malibu and parked in front of our new home. We had taken the house on the advice of Chantal's manager, Chris Kerr, who'd grown up in LA. I was able to see it in person a few months earlier, when OLP rolled through Los Angeles on a tour supporting our *Spiritual Machines* album. The place was big enough to hold a few suitcases, a bed, and not much else. When the wind blew, it felt like the walls gave up. Sand would fly around the main room and find its way into our sheets and couch. The air was moist, the waves never stopped, and for a while it was perfect. It was a reset, a rebirth.

Being in LA and Hollywood paid off almost instantly. Within the first couple of weeks there we found a great little sushi joint called Zuma Sushi. The kitchen in our place wasn't great, so we found ourselves eating out a lot. One night we must've been talking about music at the sushi bar, because this professional-looking lady sitting next to us, eating by herself, leaned over to ask if we were in *the business*. A couple of bottles of sake and an hour later, she commissioned us to write the opening title for *Stuart Little 2*, which she was producing. It wasn't exactly the Michael Mann or Christopher Nolan film that I dreamed of scoring, but it was a start.

To no one's surprise, that *Stuart Little* song didn't lead to any massive film projects, but we did start getting calls to do outside writing. This was a shift from our original plan, but it still allowed us to create together. For some reason we ended up at a lunch in Malibu with David Foster and his wife around the same time we started writing for other artists.

This instant access to celebrity is at once a total stereotype of LA—and true. Once you start opening doors in LA, there is no saying where they will lead or who will be sitting at a table, drinking merlot on the other side. I remember asking David his thoughts on whether this outside writing thing was worth it. His comment still sticks with me today. Without thinking he said, "Get the house. Get the car. Get the cuts."

> "GET **THE HOUSE**. GET **THE CAR**. GET **THE CUTS**."

Although I'd never looked at music from that angle, I appreciated his perspective as far as not letting the music business use you, and making sure you're using the business. This was before Spotify and all the other ways artists are marginalized in an industry built off their backs.

Coincidentally, soon after meeting Foster we received a call to write for a new show that had taken television by storm, called *American Idol*. We said yes, but almost as easily could have said no. We didn't have cable, so we were oblivious to just how big *American Idol* was. The management arm of *Idol* scheduled a few days with the winner of season one, a singer from Texas named Kelly Clarkson.

By this point we'd just moved into our first real home together in Malibu proper, away from the beach. We'd bought Peter Fonda's old place in a canyon right across from the infamous Duke's restaurant off the Pacific Coast Highway. It was impossible, with all the salt air, to build a studio on the beach in our cozy and constantly swaying

A-frame, so my first mission was to get a small studio up and running so we were actually prepared for these writing sessions. Instead of looking out over the ocean, we now looked out over the hills. It was like being in Tuscany.

Chantal wrote a song on the first day with Kelly called "Where Is Your Heart." We then wrote "Walk Away," which went on to be a big hit for Clarkson. The powers that be at *American Idol* loved us, and began sending us the winners of each season to write as soon as a season ended.

This was as far from scoring a Martin Scorsese film as I could imagine, but we were getting to work with some incredibly talented artists including Pink, Martha Wainwright and Katie Melua.

Carrie Underwood won season four, and her manager told me Carrie was a big OLP fan. She was already a big star but very down to earth. The first day she arrived at our home, which was also the day of the Grammys, she was in a pair of sweats. Just like Kelly, Carrie could sing her ass off. Chantal and I had still yet to watch *Idol*, but the calibre of singers we were working with seemed to suggest they were getting the winners right.

During the seventh season, OLP management told me an *Idol* contestant who'd made it to the final four had picked an OLP song to perform, "Innocent." David Cook talked about how much the words meant to him, as his brother had been recently diagnosed with cancer, a situation referenced in the second verse of the song. David's brother was originally the one who was supposed to audition for *American Idol*, but after his cancer diagnosis David took the audition instead. David won, and now he was at our studio.

We quickly wrote and recorded two songs for David's album, and he and I started a third idea tentatively called "Heroes." It was a big rock track, and I did a quick demo for us to live with before we met again. David must have shared the demo with his manager and A&R person. The good thing was they loved the song. The twist was that the A&R person, Pete Ganbarg, wanted to bring in another writer to add a different element to the song. I got on the phone with Pete, and he assured me Cathy Dennis would be the perfect addition to give the lyrics a slight twist and possibly add a few small melodic hooks.

I felt like I had to surrender when writing songs for other people. I wasn't going to sing them, so it was never stressful like writing for OLP. My job was to help the artists express what they were trying to say, and that liberated me from the pressure I put on myself to perfectly articulate my internal world. I was helping uncover their emotions in their personal stories, being the conduit to help achieve their visions. They weren't my stories. Those I kept sacred for my songs.

Up until that point Chantal and I had done every session together, so this session with Cathy Dennis, and without Chantal, was going to be a creative test. I knew it would feel different to inhabit this intimate space to write for David with another woman. That phrase "with another woman" kind of says it all. But I didn't realize just how much Chantal and I did not have the tools to navigate this strange part of being a songwriter/producer.

As soon as Cathy knocked on the studio door, I knew this would be trouble. She was a British songwriter, producer and actress, with an aura about her that meant trouble for me. She was unmistakably attractive, but my non-interest in Cathy wouldn't be enough for any wife to simply "be cool" with this situation. It comes back to the idea that songwriting is a very personal, intimate arrangement. It is not the sterile environment of an office. There is no formal work attire. You don't professionally sit around a table all prim and proper. Instead, there is a comfy couch that can be curled up on, the lights are low, the vibe is immaculate, and the purpose is to open up—accelerating the natural pace of getting to know a person.

My hope was that Chantal wasn't around or wouldn't bother coming into the studio. But before I could really get to know Cathy at all, Chantal walked in.

I immediately got this feeling in my belly that I was somehow having an affair in plain sight. Nothing could have been further from the truth. With a caring smile, I tried to present to Chantal that I was acknowledging how uncomfortable this was. As much as I had hoped it would potentially absolve me of any guilt or confrontation, it didn't.

We had yet to go to a couples' class or workshop. We hadn't navigated any sort of conflict with much skill. I remember this fear of failing as a husband, as a partner, though I wasn't able to verbalize it at that time. I could see by the look in her eyes that she was hurting, but I let my stubbornness freeze me. I got defensive and offended that she was offended, and stayed on my rolling chair in the studio, rather than going after her when she left the room.

Had I understood the concept of "being each other's healer" or "being in each other's care," I would've been able to easily diffuse any insecurities. There had to be an easier way to navigate this. I felt ill-equipped to be in a marriage, and that scared me. The thought of continuing to wing it like every marriage on my side of the family made me certain that we were destined to be another statistic—one more divorce on the Maida side.

We weren't exactly kids anymore, but we were still acting like kids, riding on the high of our chance meeting and instant chemistry. But it was becoming clear that our avoidance wasn't going to save us. Of course, it would be a few years until we acted on these quiet instincts. Lucky for us, that was the first and last Cathy Dennis session.

MY HUSBAND THE PRODUCER

I am only being slightly hyperbolic when I say I could write a melody or a song twenty-four hours a day, seven days a week, 365 days a year. At this rate it is impossible for me to personally release every song I write. This surplus of writing energy naturally created an opportunity for me to peddle songs to other artists, although I was very conflicted about doing it at the beginning.

There are two ways that you can write songs for other people. You can write a song on your own, then hurl it in the direction of someone through a label, publisher or friend. Or you can sit down and attempt to do it together with the artist.

When you write with somebody, it's intimate. Especially when you are highly sensitive and easily take on the baggage of the person you're trying to embody. It is risky emotional work, and I have been hurt by people who are disingenuous, especially early in my career.

Raine has suggested that I find a way to be more strictly business, a way to make less of an emotional investment, to build a buffer between my guts and theirs. This has always felt nearly impossible for me. The process

> "THE IDEA THAT I COULD GO INTO A ROOM WITH AN ARTIST AND NOT FEEL INVESTED IS QUITE SIMPLY UNREALISTIC FOR ME."

of cowriting *is* the sharing of guts. Songwriting is never just business for me. Even when it is, it isn't. Songwriting has always been a way to express a real experience, a way to release the real pressure of a feeling. The idea that I could go into a room with an artist and not feel invested is quite simply unrealistic for me. On many occasions I've thought that someone was a fast friend, until the job ended and the relationship spontaneously died along with it. It's easy in the intimacy of a songwriting session to forget how transactional it is, an intimate exchange with a beginning, middle and end.

My first significant songwriting collaboration was with Avril Lavigne. Both Raine and I were heavily involved in her second album, and once it came out, we exploded onto the scene as writers/producers. Labels were throwing artists at us to work with and develop a sound.

I will admit that I was not the chillest of cowriters while working with my husband. The structure of a songwriting session is so odd and personal. It's this strange lawless world full of gorgeous young women expressing their deepest feelings and fears and hopes and desires in the most intimate settings. In windowless studios, in shorts or crumpled up on couches, splayed out on beds in guest houses.

One time our publisher sent a Russian Playboy model to work with Raine for an entire weekend while I was away doing shows. It was a wise choice to set up the sessions while I was away. At least then, Raine would have a chance at having a successful week. At that point, if I was in the room with him writing for some young angel-faced cherub, I would just snap. I just did not have the skills to navigate my jealousy while gifting all my life force to the blossoming career of some young gorgeous woman beside my husband.

One time a girl came over and her cleavage was borderline graphic, and I just couldn't get past it. Women can and should wear whatever they want, whenever they want, but I was not operating at my highest frequency here. I succumbed to my lowest self and became passive-aggressive and mean toward Raine. Afterwards he was like, "What the hell were you doing?"

The music industry is not suit-and-tie. Thank God for that. It's not a normal job or workplace. We can both celebrate it for its nature, while acknowledging that it is unusual and has the power to pull up feelings that need to be recognized and handled. Feelings that, left unhandled, can be deadly to a relationship.

I have written with dozens of male artists over the years, and they often come with a gaggle of gorgeous women, draped over couches and partying in the common room of a studio complex, waiting for the person I was working with to be finished. Clearly, this is unusual for a workplace. And when that workplace was in my house, in my studio, with my husband with whom I had yet to go to therapy, it just felt a little dangerous. So my attitude was terrible. I would always try to start each session with a good attitude, but I just couldn't fake it. I am a professional feeler. That makes lying hard.

The first time Raine and I worked together as performers was for charity. I played on his songs, and he played on mine. This was probably the first time we noticed just how well we played together. When we weren't focusing on another artist and we were really leaning into each other, we clicked.

ROW

By the end of my first pregnancy, I could fall asleep, but I couldn't stay asleep. My body woke me up with demands that weren't mine. Demands to shift and turn and adjust, to get cooler or warm up.

At this stage in the pregnancy, I spent a significant portion of every night just lying there, thinking about the baby and all the terrible things that could happen. I had already been pretty carried away making sure the nursery was perfect, that the crib had the regulation bumpers installed just right, and that we had the right number of swaddling blankets for our baby boy. I was prepared, even hyper-preparing, and so nothing was left but to let your mind wander, collecting nightmarish scenarios, an ever-fattening list of things that could go wrong.

I began to worry about him. Not the baby getting out of my body, or that he wouldn't have ten fingers and ten toes. I imagined and worried about him in other iterations: the schoolboy who could get bullied; the man who could maybe join the army and go on a tour in a far-off land or go into combat; the soul who could be let down by life as an adult, maybe have the worst happen to him, become sick or lose a partner to a tragedy. It was awful.

We had just moved up a winding canyon road, into a beautiful house in Brentwood. Raine was blissed out, snoring next to me, so instead of just lying there on the torturous hamster wheel of my body's making, I went to the piano. I waddled my way to the grand and I sat down by the fire under the Mexican-themed gothic chandelier, and played "All I Can Do," a song I had written while super pregnant and unable to sleep, thinking about the life of the man I was about to birth in baby boy iteration. Raine had helped me problem solve the post chorus. I thought the end needed additional lyrics, but Raine said "Just repeat 'All I can do' and be done with it." Sometimes he knows exactly how to finish my sentences in songwriting. Now when I play the song during my live shows, it's hard to believe Row is the age I imagined he would become when I wrote it.

I always wanted to be a mother—a specific kind of mother. I made a request to God early on: *all boys, please*. Girls are terrifying. This song was my letter to my unborn first son Rowan. You give your children everything before you choose to. Your body does the giving on its own, then eventually it moves from internal to external, it moves from subconscious to conscious. I was giving this little baby everything I had, but I was giving him my worries, too, my fears of not having all the answers while trusting that he was being born into a house of love.

That night, Raine and I had a full house. Avril had moved into our hacienda in the Malibu hills to work on her album *Under My Skin*. Additionally, Raine's bandmates and producer, Bob Rock, were staying in our guest rooms along with my bestie, Stef, who was in town from Toronto to help me should I go into early labour.

The day of writing and recording for Avril's album ended with a giant dinner around our oak dining table. Once the table was cleared, Avril challenged Raine to a Jägermeister drinking contest. Raine can't let a challenge go unanswered, so as I watched the first shot, then waddled off to bed, exhausted, leaving Raine to think about his choices and consider how horrible he was going to feel in the morning. I slowly lifted my body and inched down the hall to bed. I had gained fifty-six pounds, so I was predictably uncomfortable—and couldn't have been less interested in watching my husband get demolished in front of an eighteen-year-old.

With a full house it was essential to label foods you didn't want to disappear. My name was written on the tops of the things no one was allowed to eat, not least of all the cottage cheese. It's fitting that I am completely, utterly allergic to cheese now. I ate enough for a lifetime that year.

I went to sleep knowing that I still had at least another two weeks to go. My ob-gyn was away at a weekend medical convention in Vegas. "Oh God, I am not having the baby when you're gone am I?" I exploded in her office the day before she left. She confidently calmed my terror, "Of course not. Lots of time!"

I woke up suddenly at about two thirty in the morning, as it was completely impossible to find a comfortable position at this point in a pregnancy. I was bursting out of my skin and every position felt impossible to settle into.

I leaned against the wall, relying on its stability like an old friend, as I inched out of our dark bedroom, on the hunt for cottage cheese. The lights were on bright in the kitchen, but the house was so quiet. On the way to the fridge, I noticed a clogged sink. I turned on the garbage disposal, but it didn't work. I went to the broom closet and grabbed a plunger. At this point I noticed a shot glass lodged in the garbage disposal. I started to plunge with fury.

The plunger certainly plunged something, because right there in front of the sink, my water broke and fluid shot down my leg, into my PJs. A voice in my head whispered, *It's happening.* This quiet little baby boy was announcing his presence in the outside world. He was arriving. I stumbled back to our bedroom and tried to wake up Raine, who was lying motionless, still drunk as a skunk.

I started shaking him, attempting to get more than just the subtlest signs of life. I paced around my unconscious husband while I dialled the on-call ob-gyn. She calmly told me I had time, and that I should watch for contractions.

I started panicking. This was my first child; I had no idea what was right or normal. You read books and have appointments and months of time to prepare, but still—you don't know until you know.

At this point, I was desperate to go to the hospital. I left Raine to sleep it off for a few more minutes, and went to wake up Stef and Avril. I can't remember if they were sleeping in the same room, but suddenly they were both up. They were wildly excited, though still drunk from the night before and certainly not fit to drive.

Avril was interested in being helpful, though perhaps too unmanageably exhausted and intoxicated to really assist. She did small pacing circles in the room, looking for essentials to pack in a bag for the hospital. Stef was panicked in a way that made her entirely unhelpful, too, which was funny given that she was in town to help me in case my rock star husband got completely randomly, uncharacteristically rock star-ish. We joke that Our Lady Peace was more like a Christian rock band, borderline straight-edge, well-behaved young fellows with excellent manners.

I sorted a ride with our real estate agent who lived nearby and went back to the bedroom to wake up Raine. He was so drunk. As he started to stir, he said only, "Send the fax," then drifted off again.

After some time and effort and increasing panic, I managed to get him out the door and into the front passenger seat, where he remained until we arrived at the hospital. He woke up for long enough to walk me into the hospital, then passed out again in the waiting room. I remember looking out over the ocean on the

> "I WASN'T SCARED ANYMORE."

ride down the Pacific Coast Highway to Saint John's Health Center and feeling a unique cocktail of excitement and peace. I wasn't scared anymore.

The thing that is utterly bizarre about contractions is that the time in between them is completely painless. In the stillness you think, "Oh, I could get up and run a marathon right now." I later wrote a song called "Snowing in the Desert" where I sing, "in between the earthquakes it's so calm."

But then the nurses warn you, "Okay, here comes another one," and you feel it, this truck running into you, from inside of you. The pain is so deep and otherworldly. You can't really pinpoint what is happening to you, you just enter this world of pain. You transform from a woman into a portal from one world to the next. Then inexplicably the pain stops completely, like the giant mechanical lever on the other side, the one cranking a new soul into the world, needs a break, and then it's still. The pummelling from a bat wrapped in a layer of sweaters has stopped, for now. You are no longer an animal on your knees, shocked that you're still alive. The showdown with God ends for a moment, and you think, "Oh false alarm, I'm totally fine." Then it comes again, in the same order starting with the nurse's gentle preparatory warning, "Here it comes."

I looked around for Raine as the anaesthetist entered the room. I was now almost fully dilated, and there was no point in bothering with an epidural.

"Okay, now you'll have an hour or two, because labour tends to slow down, so get some rest." I called my mom and my mother-in-law and told them the nurses' sentiments—that I could rest. I no sooner hung up the phone when I felt it again, the mechanical lever cranking from somewhere deep inside. Then the nurse said, "Maybe you need to poo, did you poop today?" I was like, "Uh, I don't know if I had a poop today, but this is not a poop."

I kept calling her back, and she made me feel like such a novice. Eventually I said, "Can you just look under the sheet please?" She did. She then ran out of the room at lightning speed and returned with my doctor.

From outside of myself I yelled, "Get my husband." As soon as my ob-gyn dashed in and looked under the blanket, she said, "Okay we're gonna do a practice push." It started again. The truck on the other side revved its engine and ran directly into me, from deep inside me. The pain was so complete that I couldn't see or hear or anything with any sort of clarity. All I could do was absorb. I absorbed the pain as I became a door, and the baby pushed down with the force of the universe.

Someone gave me a mirror to see what was happening under there. A beautiful little head, blond hair like soft feathers, then someone said, "Feel the head." I did. It was the most beautiful thing I have ever touched, so peaceful and utterly precious. He was so patient there, so vulnerable. Even in the midst of this insane chaotic entrance, he was calm and cool as we carefully pulled him out of the portal.

I pushed and screamed—a voice from an alternate universe inhabited by every woman who has given birth. Now the pain was recognizable as I approached the ring of fire. I was back on the ground in the real world where I could use words like "sting" and "burn." Then, they passed me Rowan.

I couldn't be in both places at once. I couldn't sit in my pain and ferocity while embracing the overwhelming love and victory of Rowan's face. So I did the thing mothers are so good at: I put my own pain aside and held my son. It is no wonder women so easily become martyrs. We should be fucking worshipped.

Raine appeared in the room, just sobered up enough to welcome his first born. I think Rowan's arrival was what sobered him up in the end. Avril and Stef were in the next room waiting patiently.

I guess Row wasn't breathing when he arrived, but I didn't know. They gave him all the gears necessary, this quick moving order of things happening just out of my eyeline, and then Row took his first breath. They passed him to me and Raine.

He was a mensch from the beginning, our tiny person. We knew instantly this child would wanna swim in the adult pool. He would want to sit at the adult table. You could just tell. His hair had dark roots and blond tips, as though he had just come from the salon.

We delivered the placenta—or I did, I guess. That part is a blur, but it hurt like hell. Then we went to the recovery room. Avril was the first person to hold Row. Unsurprisingly, he is kind of a rock star now, in his own way.

He came home with us the next day. I remember looking at Raine and wondering how it was possible that we got sent home with a human, a person. Like, where was the professional? This couldn't be right.

But I was like Spiderman. If Row flinched in his bassinet next to our bed I could be up and assessing in .01 seconds. I loved seeing Raine become a father. He was sober pretty much forever after that, which was very helpful because Row had colic, and the nights were rough.

We were instantly in love with this little bundle of fat and needs and love. Row developed such endearing characteristics so early in his life. He knew how to make us love him even more than we already did, which of course was the most anyone had ever loved anybody. We had a beautiful first year up in the hills, hiking and taking turns with a BabyBjörn for beautiful baby Rowan Michael Maida. It was a constant stream of friends and family in celebration of his arrival in this world, a continuous wave of exhausting bliss.

CONFLICTING PERSPECTIVES

The night Rowan was born, it was a challenge just getting to the hospital. Chantal was nine months pregnant and due in a couple weeks. OLP had rented a small studio in Malibu, not far from our home up in Las Flores Canyon. Avril was living with us at the time, and I was doing double duty producing some of the songs Chantal and Avril were writing for her second album while trying to finish OLP's *Healthy in Paranoid Times* album with producer Bob Rock.

We were all slightly burnt out, and so we decided to throw a party at our house one night for everyone to let loose a little. We barbecued around the pool, listened to Jeff Buckley and Neil Young, and the drinks were flowing.

I remember distinctly Chantal bouncing on a grey exercise ball as she mentioned she was having cramps, and the bouncing helped take her mind off it. The party continued late into the night. Bob Rock left around 2 a.m. and took a group of people with him down the canyon. Bob was the only one sober enough to drive, so everyone else was left to claim a bed, couch or lounger by the pool to sleep.

A couple of hours later I was woken by Chantal standing over me, shaking my body telling me that she was having real contractions and that we needed to get to the hospital. You would think this news would sober anyone up, but I'd drank too much and knew that I wasn't going to be able to drive. This was a problem, especially knowing that getting a taxi up to us at four in the morning would be near impossible, and there was no way Chantal could drive down our canyon made up of two miles of intense switchbacks and steep inclines.

> "IT FELT LIKE IT ALL HAPPENED IN SLOW MOTION."

Chantal had the idea to call our real estate agent, and luckily enough she answered the phone and came straight up. The next few hours were some of the most surreal of my life. Coming down the canyon and travelling along the Pacific Coast Highway as we made our way to Saint John's Health Center in Santa Monica was like a movie. It felt like it all happened in slow motion. The sun was rising over the ocean and the streets were quiet. It was as calm as any day I'd ever witnessed in southern California.

We rushed into the hospital, thanked our agent and were shown our room. This was all about to happen. Suddenly slow motion turned to real time, and there was no way I was going to not be present for my first child's birth, so I went to the bathroom and made myself throw up. I splashed cold water on my face, drank water and asked the nurse for a few Advil.

Within minutes I was alive. Holding my wife's hand. Rubbing her head and feet and trying to be as much comfort as possible. We'd done some prenatal classes, but most of it went out the window in the moment. Whatever Chantal wanted, I did too. They should have just explained that in those classes and saved everyone their time and money.

At some point there was nothing I could do to help comfort my wife. The contractions were severe, the discomfort unbearable. She wanted an epidural, so like any good husband I ran down the hallway looking for our nurse and letting her know the situation. Two minutes and two centimetres more and she would have past the point of no return for receiving an epidural, but it worked. Less than an hour after that, our first baby boy, Rowan, was born.

I used to say that writing a song must feel like what it's like to have child. I took that back instantly. Holding my newborn son in my arms while sitting next to my wife as she slept for a few minutes was as peaceful as that sunrise drive down from Malibu a few hours earlier.

If I wasn't one hundred percent sober when Rowan was born, I was now, and the clarity of realizing how any anxiety I had about being "ready" to have a child melted away instantly. No question Row was born into a small amount of chaos. Surrounded by a house full of artists and creatives the night he demanded he be released, it's no wonder he is that creative being in his own life. I saw this early on with Row. He was always sitting behind the drums in our studio or tinkering on the piano. It was rare for Rowan to walk into a room not singing. His voice and energy lit up every space he entered. As an elite basketball player in LA, Rowan differentiated himself on the court not just by his athletic ability and tenacity but by his creativity. He saw the game through a creative mind. I still keep his mixtapes from AAU ball with the Compton Magic on my phone, and I'm always amazed at how much art he had in his game every time I stumble across one of his videos. I see glimpses of how we may have imprinted on our oldest's emotional IQ. He's been on a conquest for knowledge and understanding since I can remember. Never settling. Never satisfied. Mostly, I hear it in his music. Rowan was quick to understand and channel his creativity as he started to write songs around the age of fifteen. He wasn't interested in us "helping" him with his music. He's always wanted to write his songs alone. His words. His chords. His melodies. He's deep. I do worry for him because I see myself in him often, and I know the burden you carry with that level of introspection. It's still on me decades later. It's why I continue to write songs, but that type of constant self-analysis and reflection comes with a price. And the ocean. Rowan is his mother in that sense—at one with nature. I think about that drive down from Malibu to the hospital in Santa Monica and then the serenity as we revelled along the highway and the ocean, mixed with the crazy anticipation of bringing a life into this world.

There were some early stresses that I'm sure every new parent goes through. Trying to understand how to calm your baby down, or wrap them up in those blankets to sleep properly. How long you should let them cry, or when it was appropriate to call the doctor. Chantal had some trouble breastfeeding early on, and of course there was only one brand of nipple patches that provided proper relief.

For this I often found myself in the strangest parts of LA at all hours in the morning, acting like a junkie out of a William S. Burroughs novel looking for a fix; except my particular fix was at Walgreens and was nipple patches. This could not have been any less rock n roll, but these adventures were exactly that, adventures.

TESTING A MARRIAGE

I've always heard that the top three things that test a marriage are financial problems, infidelity, and death. Never once did I think that somebody stealing your house would be up in that top three, but this is exactly what happened to us when we were living in Malibu in 2006.

We bought our first home together in Malibu, up La Flores Canyon just across from Duke's restaurant. It was a beautiful home at the end of a private lane. We only had a few neighbours around us. It was quiet and magical, as we looked out into the hills and out over then ocean.

For a kid who grew up in Etobicoke, Ontario, this was a dream come true. We didn't care that we had to drive fifteen minutes to do anything. For the first couple of years there, we hardly left the house. We were making tons of music. From OLP's *Healthy in Paranoid Times* to writing with Kelly Clarkson to Avril Lavigne living with us while we recorded seven songs for her second album, that Malibu home was a creative vessel.

The peace and serenity of things shifted with Rowan's arrival. We started to think about moving closer into town. This wasn't the only factor. I wanted to build a recording studio in this amazing barn that was on our property, but we couldn't get permits. Malibu is notorious for this.

As beautiful as our house was up in the hills, it started to feel isolated. All of a sudden that fifteen minutes just to go get diapers or groceries wasn't as romantic or easy. We'd also had a scare earlier that year, when Los Angeles got ten straight days of rain in February, and we had a huge piece of land under our deck fall away.

Chantal had organized a surprise birthday party for me. Tons of artist friends and musicians made the trek up, including Peter Hayes from Black Rebel Motorcycle Club and the singer from the New Radicals, who was painfully annoying. The talk of the party was the rain and how relentless it was. Some people were concerned about making it back down to the highway. I awoke the next morning to clear blue skies. I took my morning coffee onto the deck off our kitchen, only to notice a huge piece of the hill was gone. We immediately called an engineer to come assess this landslide, thinking it could be serious. The guy we called wasn't anyone's recommendation, just a random geological engineer we found online, and, wow, did he end up being a kook.

After a few hours of assessing the damage and structure of our house, he walked up the hill to deliver the news that our property was worthless. Literally worthless, he said. I remember looking at Chantal when those words escaped from his mouth. Our hearts dropped as we were told that the hill was volatile and could slide at any moment. He handed us a report that basically explained we should evacuate. Immediately.

Shock set in as this guy got in his little truck and drove away down the canyon. But before we let ourselves panic, we called another company for a second opinion.

Within forty-eight hours, we'd learned that the previous owner had built a vineyard on the side of the hill, and the year before we'd moved in there had been fires in the canyon. The heat from the fires had melted the PVC piping they placed underground to water the grapes, and so when it rained that year the pipes clogged, and the excess water formed pools underground—which made the hill slide. Fairly easy fix. Disaster averted. Can't say enough about second and even third opinions. Little did we know this was only a precursor to the next Malibu test.

Fact was, we did live on the side of a hill, and we started to feel the stress of that reality along with isolation being so far up Las Flores Canyon. I knew it was going to be difficult to leave that house, because we made so many incredible memories there. Lucky for us the housing market was on fire, and Malibu was a hotspot. Our agent told us we wouldn't need to list the home. She was content she could sell it through her colleagues who actively had clients looking to buy in Malibu. She wasn't wrong. A few private showings later, we had multiple offers.

The two best offers were from a professional poker-playing couple and from a retired New York Yankee named Danny Tartabull. My gut was worried the poker players could have a big losing weekend in Vegas and be forced to back out of the deal. The Yankee felt like the safer bet.

He was very charming when we signed the deal. He told us he wanted to keep the house as is. He loved all the great energy we'd created there. It was for his kids and new girlfriend, and they were excited about making a new life on the West Coast.

Unfortunately, he was full of shit. It ends up that Danny Tartabull was a professional con man. The real problem was that as soon as we began negotiations for the Malibu home, we'd purchased our new home in Brentwood. Because Chantal was pregnant with our son Lucca, we decided to have a short closing on the new house so we could move in and get settled before the baby was supposed to come.

I wasn't looking for a repeat of the drunken fiasco night we had with Rowan up in Malibu. We rushed to get packed and moved into our new home ten days after buying it. The Malibu home wasn't closing until the end of the month, but it would be fine. We left the house in immaculate condition.

What happened next is a lesson to any homeowner and, as a son of a home developer and builder, this one hurts.

Tartabull was able to convince our agent he needed the key early, before he closed, to do some minor repairs his girlfriend had noticed. Next thing we knew, our neighbour in Malibu called Chantal congratulating us on selling the home. Chantal was confused when our neighbour explained the moving trucks were there and they were moving all their stuff in. I guess our neighbour saw that as we had closed and were officially sold.

This quickly turned into a nightmare as we realized that Danny should never have had access and moved his furniture in there without closing. I knew enough from my dad and working construction as a kid that taking occupancy before closing was illegal. Now the question was, how do we get them out of there?

> “WE WERE ON OUR OWN.”

We called our agent, furious, as we realized what she had done. She put us on with the head of her firm. He told us we were in a situation that required the authorities. I knew what that meant. He was no help.

We were on our own.

We were buddies with Sean Avery, who was playing for the LA Kings at that time. I knew that he was rooming with a couple of big NHL players, so I called Sean and said, “I’m gonna write you out a contract that says that you’ve leased our home for the summer and, if you don’t mind, I’d love if you could go up to our house in your Hummer with your defencemen buddies, knock on the door, and as soon as the door opens, just bust your way in, give him the contract and tell him that he needs to leave.”

I knew this wasn’t the legal thing to do, but I also knew that if we didn’t get Tartabull out right away this was going to be a major problem.

Sean agreed to do this, and as he was getting organized, we got a call from the head of the real estate company saying that he’d spoken to the sheriff. I’m assuming Chantal had let our agent know that this was our plan. He informed me that if Sean or any of the LA Kings were to get into some type of physical altercation with Danny that he would essentially end up owning our home.

I'd always heard from my dad how squatters' rights, as ridiculous as they sound, were in fact deadly serious, and I was now experiencing this first-hand. I quickly called Sean and let him know that we couldn't go through with this plan. We spent the entire summer in court working with the lawyers, trying to evict Tartabull from our Malibu home while he threw Fourth of July parties, used our pool every day, and had a great hangout for his kids during the summer before they went back to their mom in Florida.

If we had just investigated Danny a little bit on the internet, we would've seen that he was a serial home stealer. He had done the same thing to a retired postal worker in Phoenix, Arizona, and was under investigation for similar dealings in Orange County.

While carrying two mortgages was definitely a test on our marriage, there was some sort of faith that kept us calm throughout those stressful months. A few weeks after we moved into our Brentwood home, Chantal had Lucca and we were running sessions, recording and producing out of our new home studio.

If there's a lesson I still take from that slow-moving nightmare, it is how important it is to be "in the work."

This was a philosophy originally thrown at me about music, how you always have to be honing your craft no matter what is going on outside. The music business can be nasty and try to knock you down or disappoint you, but staying present in the day-to-day allows you a better chance at survival. This is true of life and relationships.

Staying *in the work* allowed us to navigate the added chaos of having a fourteen-month-old and a newborn while going through the monumental stress of trying to evict someone. You think you'd never want all that at once, but somehow the volume actually kept us centred on each other. On a bigger goal. We had to ground each other in order to get through it.

Finally, nearly a year later, we had our day in court in Santa Monica. Chantal and I sat at the back of the courtroom. Danny didn't show up, unsurprisingly, and after our lawyer had explained the facts, the judge looked for us in the room. He said, "So I'm to understand that an ex-New York Yankee was able to get the keys to your house before he closed and live in it for several months without ever intending to pay you?"

Almost sheepishly, I said, "Yes, sir." I was so embarrassed that this could happen to us. Humiliated that we let this happen.

The judge looked directly at Chantal and I, and said, "You know what? I've never liked the New York Yankees." He slammed his gavel on that big wooden block and granted the verdict to us.

LUCCA

With Rowan, the breastfeeding was brutal. No one could sort out what was happening with my left breast, but I am stubborn. So while one of my best friends, Dr. Samantha Nutt, suggested I should “just feed on the good side,” I was for some reason determined to flow from both. It was like torture every time he latched.

What’s the point in having a women’s health specialist for a bestie if you won’t listen? I had Raine running around Los Angeles buying up these specific Gerber nipples that worked for Row. We were warned they were going to become unavailable so we bought up as many as we could find. He was like my drug dealer, exhausting every pharmacy of their stash.

Raine’s body took to parenthood like he’d been doing it all his life. He was calm and patient and would spend hours swaying with Row at night, without the dysphoria of being a malfunctioning milk machine like me. Men get to become parents without undergoing a completely disorienting physical transformation.

The ease with which Raine approached being a father was a blessing, because as any new parent will tell you, it is exhausting. Between the sleepless nights, a world turned upside down and caring for a new life, it's overwhelming at the best of times.

The first few months with Rowan were full of surprises and smirks, as his funny presence began to emerge. We loved him and the newness of our growing family.

When Rowan was nearly five months old, we left him for the first time. He stayed with my parents so we could get a weekend away. We went to this resort I had heard about from friends, called Bacara, in Santa Barbara. It was every bit as beautiful as they raved. There were lush trails, ocean cliffs and farm-to-table food. Our room had a fireplace and a Spanish feel—tile and stone, and a California king bed we collapsed onto upon arrival.

We slept and slept and then, when we weren't sleeping, we made Lucca. I was so shocked to find out I was pregnant. We had this huge world to hold on to with Rowan, and now with this new world on the way in the form of baby number two, I couldn't understand how these two worlds could possibly exist together.

How is it even possible? Rowan is just five months old, I thought to myself while pleading with the doctor for an explanation. He told me that you can most easily get pregnant after you've just had a baby. I had heard this before, but clearly the information didn't stick enough to stop us from canoodling in front of a fireplace that looked out onto lush trails and ocean cliffs.

Raine and I settled on the double-*c* spelling of Lucca because we had loved visiting the walled gothic town of Lucca in Tuscany, which we discovered on a trip to Italy while we were expecting Rowan. Raine, having grown up in an Italian community, couldn't believe I loved the name so much. He knew a hundred guys named Lucca, but for me it felt unique. It was nice to be able to refer to him by name while he was still unborn.

I thought I knew exhaustion before my pregnancy with Lucca. I would sit in my white-linen shabby chic rocking chair, very pregnant, with Rowan lying on my belly, feeding. For almost my entire pregnancy with Lucca, Row was attached to my one functioning breast. I was essentially a stick with a belly, a factory for the vitality of my sons. My body was not my own. I was probably emaciated, gaining just fifteen pounds in my pregnancy with Lucca. Everything I was eating was going to my milk for Row. Not to mention that he was wild, so when I wasn't breastfeeding, I was managing a high-energy infant.

I knew that I needed to get to the hospital quickly with Lucca. Another middle-of-the-night body alarm woke me up as I felt the contractions beginning, my water still intact. I shook Raine awake, our babysitters were summoned, and we got the heck out of the house. I was not going to risk being eight centimetres dilated before getting relief. I was traumatized from that first labour. We got to the hospital, and they directed me to go home, "You're only two centimetres dilated." I refused. "Oh no! I am staying right here. My labours move quickly."

Saint John's in Santa Monica wasn't too far from where we lived, but I did the math and by the time I got home I would be four centimetres and by the time I got back I would be transitioning. I was doomed if I left.

Sure enough, the labour started to move before they had a chance to continue encouraging me to leave. They got me an anaesthesiologist, and I blissed out for about two hours.

Raine was quietly sitting on the window ledge. I fell asleep and woke up an hour or two later to Raine and the doctor telling me it was time. I needed to push baby Lucca into the world, into Los Angeles, into our family and this life where he would become a key player.

When Rowan arrived, it was so different because they had to work on him. He arrived quiet and needed reviving to some degree, not an uncommon occurrence in the delivery room. Rowan was just over eight pounds—a full, chunky little man. Lucca, on the other hand, came out screaming to go back in. His cry was so high-pitched and loud—the kid had pipes. I thought to myself, *Wow I hope he doesn't cry as much as Row with that alarm of a voice!*

I caught a glimpse of Lucca on my left just after he came out. He was so skinny. That, coupled with the crying, made me nervous. I kept asking, "Is he okay? Is he okay?" I was reassured that he was, but it took me a minute to believe everyone. Rowan was silent when he arrived, so in my mind silent meant healthy. This was an early lesson in the immediate differences between children. Good for one isn't necessarily good for the other.

After a little while, Raine went home to retrieve Row so he could meet his baby bro. I called Tessa. I cried to her. I told her that I didn't understand how I would be able to love this brand-new baby so much and have enough love for Rowan too. I knew how much it took to love and care for Rowan. I didn't believe it was possible to do that all over again, while caring for a busy toddler.

Raine and Rowan came into the room. Rowan had grown up in one night. He was a big kid now. He had his little jeans on and was walking like a big boy. He was bashful and had learned to read the room. We held him up to the clear plastic hospital bassinet and he quietly took it all in. It was precious.

In some ways I felt like I took it all away from him in that moment, this kingdom that we had deceivingly delivered. It wasn't his kingdom alone anymore—now he had to share it.

When they say that children come out as they are, they aren't lying. Lucca was so accommodating to Row and our busy household. He was kind and patient. He hated to be cold, just like when he was born. He still hates it.

I finally gave up on my breasts and succumbed to formula. Lucca was so hungry. He drank from Rowan's big-boy bottle, which had a much faster flow. Lucca drank it back like he had never eaten in those first three months of his life.

There is no shortage of ways to bully yourself as a new mom. I felt like I had starved him with my lack of milk, and I felt like a failure for giving him formula, no matter how organic and natural. But slowly and surely, he began gaining weight, his little belly filled out, and I released myself from my own judgment.

Lucca started to grow into his sweet self, a loving little brother to Row. He would just let Rowan have the show. He would watch and learn. Something about what he saw made him a protective and caring sort. He was very empathetic and remains so. I don't have favourites, but I have always thought of him as my reprieve from chaos, good and bad.

When I had Row there were so many baby showers—one in Winnipeg, one in LA and one in Toronto. Avril was at the one in Toronto. She was so shy. I spent most of the shower worrying about her feeling uncomfortable. She was so young and so extremely famous. I guess I was both protective of her and concerned that my nearest and dearest friends and family found her presence in the room distracting. Or maybe it was me that was distracted with these two worlds colliding. With Lucca we decided to do things differently, just one shower at our LA home. My neighbour Meg threw it, and was so kind and thoughtful. I saved every card, every sweet little present, the silver rattles and teething rings.

Recently, Lucca went off to college just as I felt like I was coming up for air and ready to devote the most time to him ever—and then he was gone. It really is that fast: born, screaming, hungry, easy, and then gone.

> "IT REALLY IS THAT FAST: **BORN**, **SCREAMING**, **HUNGRY**, EASY, AND THEN GONE."

LUCCA

Having a family with Chantal changed me in unimaginable ways. I understand having a family is not for everyone, but I always knew it was something I wanted. After marrying Chantal I knew it was destined to be with her, but I had an insecurity about being ready. Truth is, you're never ready. Having a child or children is not something you can prepare for, because the changes are so profound. The changes in you, your partner and your responsibilities moving forward once you have kids, are all something to be enjoyed in real time—and not because they're all particularly inspiring or easy. It's a challenge.

Sixteen months after Rowan was born, we had Lucca. We were careful to not have any parties close to the due date. Lucca was born in the same hospital as his brother, although Saint John's had renovated their maternity ward since Row was born, so the experience felt as new as holding Lucca for the first time. We were pros by now, so we were barely in the hospital for twenty-four hours before we brought Lucca home.

He wasn't early but he was skinnier than Rowan and was released into this world with a loud scream as his long gangly arms and legs reached out to his mom. He calmed down immediately as Chantal held him.

That calmness remains. We chose the name Lucca from our trip to Italy when Chantal was pregnant with Rowan; we drove through Tuscany and stopped for lunch in the town of Lucca. To this day it's one of our favourite places in Italy, a magically preserved town that oozed heart and charm. It was impossible to not let that character wash over us as we spent a day there and the feeling stuck. A name meant for a boy as charming, genuine and kindhearted as his namesake.

Lucca is that anomaly. He is the son that other parents, teachers or coaches write or call you about in private, professing how wonderful he is. I'd like to say that we had some influence on this incredible kid. I often wonder if Lucca was somehow omnipresent through the making and editing of our documentary. I wonder if he'd secretly listened in to Chantal and me as we worked on our communication skills while he was growing up. The truth is, some kids are just born this way. His self-awareness and empathy for others are special. We'd also all agree that without Lucca, none of our dogs would have lived long lives. We've had dogs as part of our family since the boys were young, and every time the driveway gate would open without someone paying attention, our dogs would bolt out into the canyon. Undeterred by traffic, they would take off down the street as fast as they could. Time and again, he was the only person attuned or aware of these crises, and ultimately it would be Lucca chasing after the dogs in his bare feet, 400 metres down our street, saving their canine lives from oncoming cars, pickup trucks and trash collectors. Oftentimes, Lucca has been our bridge for human connection and understanding in our family. I'm not sure if this is right for the child to be that unlocked, but I'll take it. Chantal and I often reaffirm to each other how a child's brain isn't fully developed until their mid-twenties, mostly as a coping mechanism when any of our kids mess up, but Lucca, as a young child, had the code. He had the hardware functioning to always reach toward another person's pain. I struggle with how we, as adults, learn to temper empathy. We do it socially, professionally and emotionally. It's a coping mechanism in its own right. Lucca's ability to simply act is profound. I am consistently blown away when I witness this in action. I've always tried to infuse a sense of empathy in my lyrics. Lucca does it in real life. I don't think I could be more enamoured or proud.

Having two young babies and having just moved from Malibu closer to the city felt like a dream. We had abandoned the harrowing drive up and down the canyon. It became too much, especially with all the times I was sent off to Walgreens with Rowan.

We had finally gotten the Yankee squatter out of our Malibu home, and our lives were for the first time starting to feel slightly civilized. I can say honestly that up until that moment we'd felt like nomads. Always travelling, consistency was abnormal for us.

TIMING

I was sitting on the patio of the Thompson Hotel with a friend one lovely summer evening while visiting Toronto. It was warm, the gorgeous Ontario sky painted behind the umbrellas on the patio asking like always, *Should I rain, or should I hold back the tears and just keep it a humid evening?*

As we sat without thought or expectation, Monika said, "Oh wow, there's Drake. Right behind you."

I looked, then got up and walked up to him. He was so kind and friendly and comfortable in his skin—which was refreshing, given the fame and momentum he'd gained in recent months. He said he was so happy to meet me, and that he was a big fan.

We agreed we should collaborate. He asked what I was up to that night, if I would go to the studio and work on a song with his producer—and that he would get there soon, too.

In my memory, the live room was large and the control room smaller. Drake's producer, Noah "40" Shebib, and I worked out a basic part for Drake to throw ideas on. I went into the vocal booth wearing a white

T-shirt I loved that eventually got a mysterious mark on it that I couldn't get out.

I managed to pull my headphones down oven the knitted hat I wore, rather than taking it off and thus exposing my hat hair. It was a lucky instinct, given that I now know I was being filmed the night that "Over My Dead Body" was born.

When Drake showed up at the studio, I was really pumped because I knew that 40 and I had something great. I just wanted to keep singing it over and over. A very good sign. Drake had no problem getting down in the dirt with me to really figure this thing out. Most everything he said and suggested was perfect, as though he already knew the answer but didn't want to make me feel bad. He was a great collaborator, and the camaraderie was truly epic.

We ended up doing a couple of songs. I haven't gone back and listened to the other one in a while. He never focused on it. Drake can be incredibly mysterious, but he knows what he likes.

He knew how to work and be light about it, and have fun while making records. His boys were his bros. They knew what was going to happen. They knew they were witnessing something massive incoming. I can see that now, because he filmed that first night at the studio without telling me.

The video recently went viral, and I honestly didn't know how to feel. There I was. It's this little time capsule. Me after two kids, but still so damned young and naive. So innocent before so many of life's future challenges.

Drake and I talked about the video recently. I assumed he leaked it though that fact wasn't revealed in our communications. He just thought it was an awesome thing—the nostalgia, and the response from the fans.

Months later, I walked into the control room at our home in LA when it was clear the song was a winner. Raine was on the couch. He could have been right in the middle of something, but he stood up and hugged me like it was the most important thing in the world.

There are always professional peaks and valleys, but Raine is my "always."

Raine isn't a cartwheels-and-handstands guy. He is stoic, but he celebrates when he sees me really feeling a sense of achievement. I can show him the catharsis, and he can hold space for my wildest rollercoaster of emotional journeys.

> "HE CAN HOLD SPACE FOR MY WILDEST ROLLERCOASTER OF EMOTIONAL JOURNEYS."

"Over My Dead Body" was the first song recorded for Drake's massive album *Take Care*.

Who could have ever known the impact it would have? I watch his audience sing it with him in crowded arenas packed with tens of thousands of people. I see it being celebrated online by millions and millions of people, and I have to pinch myself. But I am not sure what it would mean without Raine. Without a witness, it's kind of like it never happened.

WAR CHILD

There is nothing more powerful than travel. As a child my family travelled back and forth to Acapulco every March break. My grandmother on my dad's side had a condo right off the beach, and we made a lot of great memories there. Long plane rides and vacations were always an oasis for me to consume music. I wore out cassette tapes of Van Halen's *1984*, Bruce Springsteen's *Nebraska* and U2's *Unforgettable Fire*.

Fast forward to 2000, and Chantal and I found ourselves at a dinner in Toronto with Samantha Nutt and Eric Hoskins. They were both physicians by trade, though Eric had worked in politics as senior policy adviser to Foreign Affairs Minister Lloyd Axworthy. Their latest focus was founding War Child, an international NGO serving war-affected children around the world.

I'd later find out the dinner was a setup. Chantal had already met with Sam, and the master plan was to get me to agree to travel to Iraq with War Child. A few bottles of wine later and I was intrigued. Iraq had been devastated by the First Gulf War, and the bigger NGO community had essentially ignored the country and the children suffering from the immeasurable destruction and PTSD from witnessing such atrocity.

Typically, I would sit on an idea of such consequence, but watching that First Gulf War playout on television like a video game disturbed me to my core. I remember watching the first bombs drop, devastating cities through the keens of night vision, leaving nothing but wreckage once the sun came up. It was unthinkable.

The idea of being a part of something bigger than myself was instilled early on through music. I saw Peter Gabriel perform at Maple Leaf Gardens in the early nineties. Gabriel was a fierce social activist and wore it on his sleeve during the concert. I walked out holding a Greenpeace sticker and signed up to Amnesty International.

Even before that, Live Aid in July 1985 proved to the entire world how powerful music was in making real change. U2's performance that day was seared into my brain as one of the most career-defining moments, when Bono put the world on his back for twenty minutes and made us all pay attention. Ironically, Bono would shout out Chantal and me from the stage at a U2 concert in Toronto years later, having heard about the work we'd done with War Child.

I agreed to the Iraq trip. As much as I was interested, it was Chantal who truly got me to do it—though she didn't have to explicitly say anything. Her reverence for others both near and far has always been a spell I cherish.

From the first few times we hung out, she's always humbled me. Chantal speaks so clearly on the causes she supports. Whether she is talking about her Indigenous or Ukrainian roots, her passion and empathy is humbling because her understanding and conviction magnifies every thought.

My family wasn't thrilled with the idea of me going to Iraq. I can't blame them. My mom was extremely concerned. I'd be lying if I didn't admit I shared some of that concern, especially as the trip grew near and we started to receive security briefings ahead of our departure. Eric assured me that we had a fantastic "minder" named Mike from Lebanon. Eric had been to Iraq multiple times as a physician, and he oozed a calm confidence.

Mexico had its problems back in the day. We'd routinely seen military patrolling the Acapulco beaches with AK-47s and witnessed cartel violence, but Iraq was an actual war zone. We landed in Baghdad aboard a UN plane. Mike met us at the airport and helped the Iraqi ministry of information process our visit.

> "THE STRESS LEVEL REMAINED HIGH THROUGHOUT THE TRIP."

The stress level remained high throughout the trip. Our hotel rooms were bugged, and every move we made needed to be cleared by the ministry of information. The call to prayer was an intimidating but comforting daily routine, even though there were multiple times when I legitimately thought our lives were in danger.

I learned more about the world on that trip then I had in all my years before. We stood at the Tree of Life where the Euphrates meets the Tigris. It was profound. We couldn't help but realize in that moment the smallness of our existence.

I'd later travel with War Child to Darfur in 2004 and then Afghanistan in 2025. Equally harrowing trips. Equally eye opening. In 2025 I was honoured with the War Child founder award. To say that War Child has changed millions of children's and families' lives would be an understatement. Dr. Samantha Nutt is a testament to what moral imagination can achieve when matched with persistence. The irony is I am one of those lives they changed.

SAL

My pregnancy with Sal happened after a trip to Ethiopia with War Child. Raine and I have been working with the organization for nearly fifteen years, and every journey has been beautiful and challenging and humbling in its own way, but this one brought me to new levels of emotional exhaustion.

For me and Raine, having a platform in and of itself didn't really feel like enough anymore. I felt a level of compassion I didn't know how to move through. Having children had heightened the desire to give back with more urgency than ever before.

With some love, you can easily find a full and complete way to act on it. You feel the wave, then make your beloved a cup of tea, or simply wrap yourself around them, or rest your head on their shoulder. With certain types of love, it's easy to get from one side to another with a simple loving gesture.

In Ethiopia I fell in love with so many children and young women and men. I didn't know what to do with it all. I didn't know how to fully express it, to feel its impact. It was this profound wave of love that had nothing to do but exist. That may be the best part of travelling to places around the world, this feeling of discovery, not only of the people and the place, the history and the politics but also the experience of your own growth. Our trips with War Child introduced both Raine and I to a love we hadn't felt before.

A young woman, Frehiwot, showed me her home in the city of Addis Ababa. She cared for her younger siblings, as their parents were dying due to the effects of HIV/AIDS. They slept on mats on the floor as Frehiwot prepared and served meals. There is a photograph of me and her in the archaic path behind the home, where she cooked outside in a coal stove. I look sad. She looks joyful. In the photo we are embracing. After the photo, we cried and embraced again. The insides of her arms were burned the way many women's were, a product of using curling irons heated up manually on those miniature coal ovens.

I remember the end of the trip, the flights out of Iraq, Jordan and Iraqi Kurdistan. I remember them with intention. I make a point to remember Frehiwot and her siblings, but it never becomes easier to leave someone hoping for better. They are not alone in their hopes for better. Everyday back home we hope for better, better in our relationships, better pay, better TVs and phones, better customer service. But the list of *better* in the places I've visited with War Child reads differently: better bathrooms in a refugee camp, better ways of cooking, better ways of passing checkpoints or shopping at markets for bread without worrying that tragedy will strike.

When I looked out the window of the airplane at the end of the trip, the guilt I felt, for the life I had, wrapped its useless arms around me and held me there. Our luck begins where we are born; our passports are golden tickets. I got home and fell into my husband's arms, my guilt shifting into gratitude for him, our walls and the roof over our head. A month later we found out Sal was on the way.

I loved every minute of being pregnant with Sal. It's not that it was less challenging than Row or Lucca, it's just that I knew he would be my

Wedding day

Young love

CHANTAL AT 7 YEARS OLD

Raine's high school band

Order of Canada ceremony

Halloween 2013

The Wonderment

Brothers

Shangri La Studio

Santa Monica Beach

Chantal dressing room SNL

Boys 2024

Niagara On The Lake

Walk of Fame 2014

Rowan, Toronto

Raine & Chantal in Iraq

Sal Perfroming with CK

JUNOS Allen Waters Award

OLP Canadian Walk Of Fame induction

CHANTAL & LUCCA IN UGANDA

Raptors v Lakers

Art show Los Angeles, Rowan & Chantal

OLP Canadian Walk Of Fame

R&C Montreal

Chantal Get To You shoot

OLP Houston, TX

Tofino

Tokyo, Japan

Eric Hoskins, Raine Darfur

Raffael Mazzuco Shoot NYC

Global Morning

OLP Victoria

Sam Nutt & Chantal, Ethiopia

David Suzuki Blue Dot Tour

Raine & Sam Nutt,
Afghanistan

Rowan opening 2023

Ontario Summer

Kyoto, Japan

Raine's Solo album

last, and so I relished every stage. Even the most uncomfortable parts were steeped in gratitude.

It was December 31, and I was the last patient at the radiology clinic for my sonogram with Sal. I was going to have him at thirty-five, though I was thirty-four at this moment, and so they needed more extensive tests. If I did well in these initial tests, I could also avoid the dreaded amniocentesis that everyone had to get back then, if they were pregnant at thirty-five and older—an archaic-looking needle inserted into the abdomen to test a sample of amniotic fluid for genetic issues.

I asked the sonogram technician if he could tell me my child's gender. He said, "Well, I can, but I am not permitted to tell you. The doctor will be in shortly." I was only twelve weeks along. We used to have to wait until eighteen weeks to know anything about the sex of the baby, but I guess the technology had improved since my other two pregnancies just a few years earlier.

The doctor came in. He told me I had the uterus of a nineteen-year-old, a fact I received like he was a modelling scout calling me hot. My young uterus wasn't only flattering; it also allowed me to avoid the dreaded amnio needle. I asked him if he could tell me the sex: "Listen, I am a bit of a mess with regard to the idea of having a daughter, so I need to know what is happening, so please, just tell me?" He said, "I am not really supposed to tell you this now but you're my last patient of 2007 so here you go. See these three dots? If they were further apart it would be a girl, but because the dots are close, we know it's a boy."

I was overjoyed. It was as if it was the first time someone said "It's a boy" to me. Those words just never grow old. I would never have to face my utter terror at the thought of raising a woman, a little me. I always tell people, "If you're having girls, you're meant to."

I was crying tears of joy, and couldn't dial Raine fast enough. He answered the phone, and I yelled, "It's a boy!" He was quiet. He said, "You can't know for sure; you're not even twelve weeks along." I said, "Oh no! We know! It's a boy!" Raine took a gentle pause then nearly whispered into the phone, "Could you not have waited a little?" I heard the tempered disappointment in his tone. He told me he didn't care what the sex of the baby was, but that it was exciting to consider the possibility of a girl. It kind of broke my heart. You can know someone forever and still not know everything there is to know. It was hard to believe I had no idea that Raine relished the idea of being a girl dad. Raine can be a closed book, so because I had never asked, I never knew. It's moments like this in our life together that I find so humbling. Raine is in my care, and if I don't ask him certain things, he won't chime in and voice his feelings.

"IT'S MOMENTS LIKE THIS IN OUR LIFE TOGETHER THAT I FIND SO HUMBLING."

Our conversations often involve me asking questions, as the more naturally outgoing of the two of us. This stark difference in our operating speeds was a real challenge for a long time, until I just accepted it. I have always been the wind-up doll in our relationship, cranking the metal key sticking out of my back, turning it until it can be turned no more, then letting the floodgates open. If the conditions are good, Raine mirrors it, telling me everything I could ever want to know, offering a wave of questions and a wave of answers.

I think our differences bring us together to level each other out. I wonder if perhaps, by the end of our lives, Raine will be more like me, and I more like him.

These days, Raine will see me about to pick a battle then slow me down. He'll use these moments of calm to connect before the damage of a fight is done. Then sometimes he wants to tell me he is hurt without telling me why, then it is up to me to choose patience to slow him down to find peace.

I feel like that's his way of saying something bothers him. Sometimes, though, like the moment I told him we were having a boy, his soft heart comes through, and he expresses an "ouch" in such an eloquent and irresistible way.

A NEW REALITY

The idea of writing and producing for other artists started to make even more sense with two kids, because we could be home more. But when we had our third son, Salvador, it became an inevitability. Life would have to change.

Salvador was born at the same hospital in Santa Monica as his brothers, but he was the only one born naturally. Even so, his actual birth was much more intense than his brothers, and we spent even less time at the hospital with Sal then we did with Lucca. Clear-eyed and sober, we brought Sal home almost immediately.

Sal was calm. We joke around that Sal never really saw a doctor until he was a teenager. The thinking is that it's because we were much less uptight parents, but it had more to do with the fact that his steadiness from an early age grew with him. He was committed to keeping up with his brothers from day one. Sal's competitive spirit is unique. To be measured, as Sal is, is not to be confused with calm. Calm can be a performance. What I've learned over the years is that being measured is something deeper and less visible. It has an internal architecture that can hold both effort and acceptance, without one cancelling the other out. For a teen of Sal's age, I find it extraordinary and genuinely hard. My nervous system can hardly manage this, but an adolescent nervous system is not designed to be measured. It goes against the grain of their own biology. And yet Sal has always been able to. Since I can remember, he's been able to navigate situations with more maturity than most adults I know. He was the first athlete to let a high-level basketball coach know his methods of getting in players' faces and screaming at them were juvenile, and he wouldn't have any part of it. He told us matter-of-factly, at twelve years old, that he was walking away from that program because he wouldn't let the fear of that coach be a referendum on his identity. Chantal and I were shocked but incredibly proud. He's never been shy to confront teachers and school officials about injustices he sees in class or in the yard, and he's handled these situations with a measuredness that's often spooked the adults in the room. Needless to say, we've sat in the principal's office on multiple occasions listening to them try to absolve or justify their mistakes in front of a child. It would be easy to just say Salvador is an old soul. He probably is, but I also think some of his God-given traits have allowed him to evolve on a unique timeline. Sal, like Chantal, has perfect pitch. He sings beautifully and at eight years old had already performed in front of thousands of people with Chantal at her Christmas concerts, singing both solo and harmonies with his mom. Measured. With his natural ability, you'd think he'd be super thirsty to leverage it to some sort of fame. Nope. His perfectionism and competitiveness have never come at the expense of decency. I'm not sure whether this is learned behaviour or if he arrived at it independently, but it's a lesson that Sal keeps giving. He is a constant. A true treasure of a young man.

I swear Chantal willed three boys, knowing she didn't ever want to have a version of herself to raise in a daughter. I would have been fine either way, but my dream was complete.

I loved these boys so much that the idea of missing any part of them growing up was the only real stress in my life. We spent so much time together as a family in these early days. When any of our boys woke up in the middle of the night, we turned it into a party. It was just another opportunity to hang out together. Rarely did it feel like a burden being up at 3 a.m. with one of the kids. There was no question we were sleep-deprived for a few years straight, but we were fortunate to be able to do that.

This new reality made for a difficult balance with OLP. I could not continue the same recording and touring schedule as before. Luckily, bassist Duncan Coutts had started a family of his own and also had three kids, so there was strength in numbers—but nevertheless an adjustment. We made the next few records in Los Angeles at my home studio. There were a few reasons why this worked for the band, but I was grateful being able to be so close to my kids while we wrote and recorded.

“THIS NEW REALITY MADE FOR A DIFFICULT BALANCE WITH OLP.”

I was compelled to make two solo records during this same time, as I started to realize that my children would probably get to know me through my words and songs more than anything I'd ever sit them down and explain or tell them. This realization brought with it a great weight, and those two records, *The Hunters Lullaby* and *We All Get Lighter*, were a direct reflection of wanting to express who I was, without the collaboration or filter of Our Lady Peace.

If music was the evidence of life, I needed to make sure my voice, my thoughts, my ideals, moral code and dreams were crystallized through these solo albums.

THE HUNTERS LULLABY

By the time Our Lady Peace finished our deal with Columbia Records around 2005, technology changed the way music was distributed. Apple launched its digital sales platform on the back of Napster and peer-to-peer streaming.

I would have been panicked not having a label for support earlier in my career, but what was happening in real time was a democratization of an industry. The gatekeepers were now being threatened. Their grip on who succeeded and who didn't was slipping.

For those of us artists not immediately terrified by change, this was a good sign. Even though my experience was positive with Sony and the execs who signed us, all the way up to Donnie Ienner, the president of Columbia Records in NYC, this was not the case for all my peers. The shift allowed artists to take back control of their creative futures.

Unfortunately, with every new technology there is always a downside. One was that a lot of the good people we'd come up with were losing their jobs. This paradigm shift meant consolidation, and it wasn't just the major labels losing money, but also some of the influential indie labels were hitting rough waters. That meant the beginning of the end of record labels spending money on developing artists like OLP. Of course, there were a few exceptions, with bands like Arcade Fire or Interpol breaking out, but generally speaking, the new music coming out was unapologetically signed and released to claw back the profits that were being lost to digital. The music business was changing, and I needed to change with it.

I'd never call myself a spoken-word artist, although the delineation between poetry and music was always fuzzy in my mind. I'd considered Leonard Cohen a poet first. Artists like Mos Def and A Tribe Called Quest were poets who just also happened to be successful in mainstream hip hop. Their influence led me to discovering more underground artists like Saul Williams, Anis Mojgani and Sage Francis. At this point in my growth as an artist, the work of these wordsmiths became singular in their creative impact on me.

The music was too profound to ignore. Sage would say more in one song than other bands on entire albums, words that were timely, raw and powerful. Listening to songs like "Sea Lion" or "Broken Wings" was like digesting an entire film in four minutes.

I went deep down this rabbit hole—obsessed. It completely changed the way I wrote. Instead of picking up an acoustic and crafting stream-of-consciousness melodies while I fumbled through different chord progressions, I started making beats. An alt-rocker raised on R.E.M., Springsteen and U2 was now sitting in front of an 808, programming until the early hours of the morning.

I'd then find the right cadence to sing while composing pages and pages of prose. The trick with Our Lady Peace was always trying to condense words and thoughts. Say as much in as little as possible was the rock-n-roll game. This wasn't that.

> "I WENT DEEP DOWN THIS RABBIT HOLE—OBSESSED."

Describing why we moved to California wasn't supposed to be condensed into a short catchy verse. Explaining what I might do if I found myself involved in a convenience-store robbery was never meant to be edited down to a few lines and a chorus. I was desperate to create a palette that would provide the foundation for lyrical and rhythmic exploration—to express expanded ideas and stretch my ability to communicate complex feelings.

As I became steadfastly focused on this new pursuit, Chantal became my muse. I'd ask her into the studio after a song was starting to take shape and have her play dark, jazz-influenced chords. She became part of this sound. I'd ask her to sing haunting harmonies or create these beautiful vocal pads referencing old Elvis or Sinatra arrangements.

The process was incredibly liberating and terrifying at the same time. The more I wrote, the less I felt I knew where this music could exist. I was fairly sure OLP fans would hate it, but this was also validating in a strange way. The thought of making a solo record that would have impinged on anything Our Lady Peace had created felt cheap. I'd always hated artists who made a lighter version of the band they were in. I never understood the point.

I felt like I was going out on a serious limb here, and about to get crucified for trying something that had its roots in spoken word. My self-critic labelled my exploration as pretension. Whatever the outcome was to be I couldn't not do it. I held to that Bowie quote about it not being art if it didn't make you scared, or something like that.

The Hunters Lullaby was released in May 2007 on Nettwerk Records. I was officially an independent artist on an independent label.

The idea of performing this music live was as terrifying and exhilarating as making the music, but going out on tour was to be the ultimate manifestation of this vision.

The tour was a family affair. Chantal, our young boys and our nanny, Heather, joined. Kevin Fox was on cello; Randy Cooke on drums. A friend of mine, Jared Paul, a spoken word poet from Rhode Island, rounded out the bus.

Jared was opening the shows with a thirty-minute spoken word set, born out of the Rhode Island scene under legends like Sage Francis. Jared was, for all intents and purposes, a militant. He wore a uniform of vintage army jackets and ripped blue jeans. He was an anti-capitalist, a vegan who did his best to convert others on the bus, but also a super bright and gentle soul.

So off we went, travelling across North America like some ragtag Partridge Family.

The shows were amazing. The crowds incredible, but the highlights were the late-night conversations Jared and I would have on the bus as we crossed the frozen highways trying to figure out the world, or at least our place in it.

Our bus driver at the time was also Springsteen's bus driver, and told us stories of how Bruce would also sit up front either with his son or some other band member and have deep conversations that went well into the morning. In a way it felt like this was a rite of passage.

Each night Chantal would open the thin wood door that separated the bunks from the front lounge and try to drag me to bed. As I'd pry myself away from those conversations, Jared would relay the same words, "Big Raine, celebrate the small victories brother, celebrate the small victories."

It became a bit of a mantra for the tour, but I never realized what it really meant until much later. It's easy to get so caught up in what's next that you forget to be in the moment. This has been a problem of mine since I can remember. I've always been so focused on what's next, what's the next song to write. What's the next show we're playing, next tour, next week off.

Having children helped, but even the phrase "being in the moment" felt like some corporate marketing cliché designed to get me to buy a timeshare in the Caribbean. What Jared was taking about was falling asleep with your kid, talking to a fan after a show or having a meal with Chantal. This thoughtfulness was poignant coming from a tough Rhode

Island kid who poetically dismantled institution after institution each night on stage. He was a bigger contradiction than me.

To inspire a crowd with only words and cadence and one body is a gift. To sit side stage and witness this night after night, also a gift. Jared was resilient. Not every audience appreciated his set, but the cities that got him, got him.

Celebrate the small victories.

EUROPEAN TOUR AVRIL

In 2002, OLP toured Europe with Avril Lavigne. We were gone for a while, and being fourteen hours and an ocean away from home is much different than simply being in Boston or Montreal and just five hours from LA. For whatever reason this tour was a little more rock n roll than most. I've always been a "your body is your temple" kinda guy. This stemmed from my parents, who were always active.

I studied martial arts growing up, and I tried to keep that practice on the road as much as possible, so really indulging in drugs or alcohol never seemed to work for me. This tour was different. The band was on a high—literally and figuratively—as our album *Gravity* debuted at number seven on the *Billboard* charts. It was our highest-charting album, and it felt great to be out there playing to new fans and performing new songs.

The indulgences seemed to get heavier as the tour went on. By the time we made it to London, my communication with Chantal had become noticeably dysfunctional, strained for no reason other than the distance and disconnection.

It all fell apart during the last show of the tour. At the afterparty, the champagne was flowing, and I drank way too much. I remember stumbling back to my hotel and calling home. This was an extremely ill-advised call. It turned out to be a terrible incoherent conversation—a call with no intention that drunkenly stumbled into a near breakup. For whatever reason I'd told her that the stress of our lives was too much, and she'd be better off without me. This was beyond selfish and stupid, and it was definitely the alcohol speaking, but I was about to board a plane and was twenty-four hours from landing in Los Angeles. No phone call or text was going to repair the damage done. I was sick the entire journey home, running back and forth to the bathroom. There is nothing more disgusting than throwing up in a plane bathroom. And I was sure this was only the beginning of my penance. When I wasn't in the bathroom, I sat gutted, staring out the window into the clouds, looking for answers, trying to piece together the conversation we had. I couldn't exactly remember everything I said, so my mind raced with different thoughts about how bad the damage was.

When I finally got home, I realized I'd said some truly hurtful things, the idea that we shouldn't be together any longer being the worst. I didn't mean it, but there I was, faced with Chantal looking at me wondering what the fuck had just happened.

Trying to play it off as a drunken moment wasn't good enough. She knew those thoughts don't simply come out with a few drinks. This was obviously something I had been thinking about, and the alcohol just gave me the courage to say it out loud. Thing is: this wasn't true. This confession was born out of my insecurity that I wasn't good enough for our relationship. I'd felt that I was letting Chantal down, so forcing what felt like an inevitable breakup felt like part generosity and part defence mechanism.

We sat on our deck looking out over the Malibu hills for hours, trying to unfold the crisis while holding on for dear life. We talked. We sat in silence. We cried. We dissected every nuance of a relationship that wasn't overtly in crisis before I left for Europe. The prospect of breaking up was terrifying.

What I realize, looking back on that moment, is that we didn't have the tools to navigate that conflict properly. Our life had been happening so quickly since the day we met. We had never taken the time to figure out how to properly communicate. More important, in this particular situation, we wouldn't learn until much later how your brain starts to move into a state of independence after being away for more than two weeks from your partner. Knowing this, especially in an occupation with so much distance built in, is vital; the crossroads we found ourselves at, unbeknownst to us, undoubtedly had that element driving it.

It took some time, but we didn't give up. Against all my good sense, I left for Hawaii soon after returning home: OLP was scheduled to begin working on our next album with Bob Rock at his studio there. Everyone was eager to keep the *Gravity* momentum, so we were locked to record. Flights, hotels and the studio were all booked.

It was not the best time for me to leave, but I would use these sessions as a vehicle to explore my thoughts and the pain of what Chantal and I were going through. My lyrics were heavily influenced by this crisis; songs like "Apology" and "Bring Back the Sun" were born out of it. My hope was that lyrics like "You, you're the air I breathe, I'm the lock, you're the key" and "Bring back the sun, let's bury this hate, fill it with love" would help make my case. If music was the evidence of life, these songs would be the evidence of love and absolution.

Chantal came to Maui while we were recording, which signified a sort of healing, or beginning at least. That *Healthy in Paranoid Times* album was born out of me almost falling apart and being resurrected by both my young family and music.

Charles Bukowski has a great quote: "You have to die a few times to truly live." Personal growth and the search for meaning often require a series of transformative experiences, challenges or even failures.

A part of me definitely died over this, and the experience left an indelible mark on my soul. Now we collectively try to limit consecutive number of days away touring.

THE LAST BIRTH

A friend of mine was a huge proponent of all-natural births. At the time of my pregnancy with Sal, Ricki Lake had just made a documentary about the cost of birthing in hospitals, the up-costs and unnecessary services leading to nonessential drugs and C-sections. She insisted that I watch it. Experiencing that documentary cemented a decision I had already been leaning toward.

Before settling on the name Sal, I had been up north to my ancestral home of York Factory near Churchill, Manitoba, where I had met an elder named Flora, whom I adored. She said she would do some dreaming and give us our baby's name.

After three excruciating weeks, she offered this long, beautiful, ancestrally packed northern/Indigenous name. I was so excited to reveal the name to Raine, but I knew I had a big sell here. Raine loved two-syllable names, simple, trim, easy to remember, RoWan, LuCca, ChanTal. The name Flora shared was long and Ojibwe and hard for even me to pronounce.

We hung up the phone and I thought, *Hey those last three syllables of the ten are interesting*. I sat Raine down and said, "What about we call him Wawatay and then we can just call him Tay for short? That way there is an ancestral honour, but his main name is easy-peasy." Raine didn't hate the name Tay so we were getting somewhere.

Then one afternoon we were sitting with our friends Sam and Eric in their Toronto home. Eric asked how we were doing on the hunt for the perfect name. I told him we would end up with Tay from the Wawatay thing, and with his razor-sharp yet subtle wit, he quipped, "Oh great, so his name is TayMaida, like tomato." This is why it is all at once dangerous and informative to share the name of your unborn child with family and friends. We pivoted to Salvador.

Sal was going to be my last birth, and I wanted to feel everything. I wanted to bring this little guy in as naturally as possible. I was no longer scared, and with the new closeness I was feeling to my ancestry, I wanted to honour a tradition my dear Auntie Pat informed me about. She was a nurse her whole life in Selkirk, Manitoba, where my grandmother was born and raised her family. She learned from Indigenous ladies who birthed naturally and in silence. A new and beautiful challenge struck me.

Raine had just one gig booked a few weeks before the expected due date. I felt a repeat coming on from when Rowan was born, while my ob-gyn was away at a conference in Vegas. I desperately didn't want to deliver without Raine. I had a small condition that was increasingly excruciating throughout my pregnancies, and worse with each one.

I went to the doctor to describe the pain I was in and make sure Sal was okay. She couldn't believe how intense my pain had gotten: "Enough. We need to get this little guy out."

She stripped my membrane in her office. This was the most painful thing I have ever experienced in my life, besides breaking my femur.

Within the next forty-eight hours, Sal was out.

The birth itself was the greatest moment of my life. My water had broken in the evening, and we walked into the hospital while I was three centimetres dilated. The nurses asked what my birth plan was. Raine said we would like no intervention, unless requested. I intervened saying that may not be true, and Raine insisted it was true. He very much supported me in my commitment to do this birth completely naturally.

I remember that there was a lady next to me in her room, at two centimetres. She was moaning so much. They said that she had already been in labour for twenty-four hours. I waited for the pain to strike me to the point of my own brand of animal grunting and moaning. I did my labour silently. I rocked back and forth at the end of the bed in our basic hospital room.

Raine sat on the windowsill, waiting for commands, until he noticed me looking like I was going to vomit. I felt Sal move down my body. It felt like getting punched in the gut for five minutes straight.

By the time Raine requested a bucket from a nurse, Sal had given up the gut punching. I was stoic until, during an intense bout of nausea, the team came in to check on me. They asked me to get on the bed. At this point it was nearly impossible to move. I guess Sal was almost at the end of his journey. I remember when they laid me on the bed, they asked me to move my leg, and it felt like I was lifting my leg over Sal. It felt unbearably painful and uncomfortable. The nurse told me I was almost done labouring.

The pressure to push was enormous, and this was something I hadn't felt during the other two boys' deliveries. I thought I was going to die, and I couldn't look at Raine. He was calm and quiet. He reassured me once, quietly, simply—and then chaos took over my mind. They told me to wait until my doctor, Maria, got there. She arrived, and I said, "Sorry Maria, I have to push, I can't wait." Out came the biggest lioness roar from somewhere that can only access itself, somewhere deep like ancestral roots, somewhere generations back—and then out came Sal.

After I delivered, Raine left for his gig. I went to sleep, and by the time I was ready to leave the hospital, Raine had returned to pick me up, flowers in hand.

We stopped for diapers on the way home. Things felt immediately simpler with Sal. Or maybe it was us who had changed now, knowing our way around a baby.

Sal was so precious, and I just loved how realized he seemed, so formed and perfect. He was a real Maida, dark hair and brows, completely adorable. He was instantly my greatest work. I felt deeply, immediately connected to him.

When we were leaving the hospital, the lady in the room next to me still hadn't delivered. I couldn't believe that they didn't provide the drugs to move her along, but like they say in Ricki's movie, upsells can lead to unnecessary C-sections.

Like Rowan and Lucca, Sal came out as himself, sharing subtle clues to who he was. Rowan is hardcore, not messing around on any level. It was almost as if he took over the room the moment he came into the world.

Lucca is a lover and just wants to stay warm. And Sal is still my little buddha baby. He is reasonable and content and completes the song. Rowan is my chorus, Lucca is my verse, and Sal is my bridge. I love them so much I could split.

Our children became the centre of our shared world. The adventure and joy and connection they have brought to my life, and the way that they bond their father and I forever, has been universe shaping. It's the oldest thing in the world, and still the most miraculous.

When your focus is solely pointing in the direction of your children's health and happiness, it is possible to forget about your own health and the health of your relationship.

Quiet resentments began building up between me and Raine without us realizing—resentments we didn't yet understand the importance of unearthing.

TESSA

As a little girl, if I could have just pushed a button and teleported myself to Tessa's house, I would have. She had amazing curly hair, big brown eyes, a tiny nose. We met at acting class and shared a deep love of movies and video games.

She was a few years older than me. I loved that she was older, like the big sister I never had. We were different, complementary. I spoke to anyone about anything, brazen as the day is long. She found socializing more challenging, yet still I felt like we were basically conjoined twins that perfectly balanced each other. We both lived in Charleswood, just ten minutes by bike. She could never be close enough, never accessible enough, ten minutes was ten minutes too many for my Tessa. I loved her family as I loved her. Her house became my house. It just kind of worked out that way. I adopted the Emery family. I think I got a little more girl energy at Tessa's because she had a little sister and growing up in my stricter, more religious house made hanging out at hers relaxing for me.

When I first saw *Stand by Me*, I wondered if it had been shot in Winnipeg. I swear to God we had that same train track, and there were definitely horrible incidents along Wilkes Avenue in Charleswood. I have always found the tracks dangerous and even possessed or something. But I would hop on my bike as a little girl and make my way all the way over to Tessa's house either on Eldridge, which was down from my house with more cars, or on Wilkes along the tracks—less cars but probably a little more dangerous.

Even though I was always pooped by the time I got to Tessa's on my bike, I walked in like I wasn't out of breath, ready to chill with my bestie.

I could sneak cigarettes and I was allowed to take Cokes out of the fridge, or so I thought. It was paradise and an opportunity to exhale.

My brother Trevor was friends with Tessa's big brother Chris and that made me feel even more comfy and connected when I was hanging out there. They played a lot of video games. Chris even held a world record in Pac-Man and Q*bert and other games. I thought that was so cool. He used to draw crowds even at the 7-Eleven on Roblin.

One time the owner of the store got annoyed because Chris's game lasted twenty-four hours or something, so he unplugged it. I think Chris was going for another record.

Tessa was my hero and the gatekeeper of her house which was my island. At her house I didn't practice piano, instead I just played whatever I wanted. I would entertain and test out my skills playing all the songs from the radio and everyone's favourite bands.

I know that Tessa had insecurities of her own, but I had her on such a pedestal. She was older than me and I think I just looked up to her so much. When we got into a tiff, and she needed space, it meant space from the whole fam jam. I felt really lost at times and alone if she and I were on the outs.

I can remember wanting to make up immediately, whereas Tessa might want a little space, reasonable enough in retrospect. Eventually we would make up and I would feel safe again. All was right with the world. Even with the age gap, we went through everything together at all the stages. I loved that she wasn't in my school friend group and I wasn't in hers. We barely ever overlapped our peers and we didn't really care. We had all the fun we needed hanging out together. Tessa was sharp and funny and compassionate and could go super deep into wild topics.

I think she got that from her mom who was such an incredibly interesting woman, and my sometimes-biggest fan. I knew I was onto something if Lynda liked a song.

I left Winnipeg around the age of twenty-two, and we remained very close. But things were different after I left. I couldn't ride over on my bike, and I couldn't tell her I would pick her up in ten minutes in my beater car my dad got me when I turned sixteen. My portable stereo was probably worth more than the car. Tess and my friendship could have lulls and space, but we still knew who each other was and that we meant the world to each other. Even though we worked at it, and she came to visit in California, and I tried to be in touch as much as I could, something happened when my boys were quite little.

Suddenly no matter what I said in texts and emails to Tessa, she found massive offense in it. Her replies took a while, and it was almost like she wasn't reading the communications I was sending. It was like she was reading a completely different email filled with insults or something. All I wanted to do was get on the bike, pedal over and sort it out.

I found out she was picking up a shift at her dad's medical clinic. That's one of those numbers in my internal speed dial, it hides in some corner of my mind along with random commercial jingles and prayers from church.

I called there, and sure enough she answered, as she always did, in this much more knowing voice, a true gatekeeper now, an adult receptionist at a busy practice, ready for anyone's BS. "Hi, Envoy, how can I help you?" barely a dip in her tone. I said, "Don't hang up, it's me." She didn't hang up. I said, "I found this place in the city that can help us. Would you come meet me if I fly in this weekend?" She paused for what felt like a lifetime, then she said, "Yes."

At that point we could have stopped the silliness. We were back on, obviously. The mere admission of desire to do some work together spoke to the main point, that we loved each other and never wanted to be on a bad wavelength again. We knew we were each other's lifelines. We were each other's superhuman heroine superstar sister from another mister. But something else was going on here. We didn't know it, but we were both being raised by the forces in our lives to be cycle breakers, critical thinkers with the ability to overcome inherited dysfunctions.

The universe didn't want it to happen organically, naturally. The universe wanted us to do the work, to earn it. I don't know if it was a Google search or speaking to someone from Winnipeg by chance, but I had found a communications-training team for office and family dynamics. They did crisis work and team building. Our coach's name was Louise. I liked her right away. Louise and her giant, red, untameable curls would get it.

As soon as I landed in Winnipeg, I rented a car. I didn't go home as I usually do. I went right to Tessa. The car ride was quiet. The sort of stillness that has the power to make me spiral out or force a thousand questions on a person who clearly doesn't want to talk. We went into this building in St. James on Saturday morning. I hadn't noticed it before, although I'd driven down this street a thousand times. It was almost as if it had grown out of the earth just for us.

We were welcomed there by Louise and another gentleman. They led us up some stairs and through a series of hallways, and sat us down in a small office and started: "What brings you here today?" When you're ready to be asked this question, it can explode the lid off boxes you didn't even realize you had sealed shut.

We spoke for two full days. We learned about each other's fears and traumas and what we meant to each other. We learned about what our words meant in our own minds and how easy it is to be misinterpreted through our individually imperfect, trigger-filled viewfinders.

It was there that I could tell Tess that she had a power and presence in my life unique to anyone in my entire world, and that with it she could take me down all too easily. And that made her all at once an invaluable and terrifying pillar in my life. It felt hard to believe that after all of the bike rides, the outcast moments, the parties and drugs, after the years of pressing our faces together, calming each other's cowlicks with random products in her parents' bathroom, after knowing every intimate detail about every guy, the first kisses and nursing each other's seemingly continually broken hearts, after everything, we actually hadn't fully understood each other after all.

> "WE ACTUALLY HADN'T FULLY UNDERSTOOD EACH OTHER AFTER ALL."

She needed to say, "I feel like I don't matter to you anymore. I feel like you needed my family as a sort of surrogate safe space more than you needed me." And I needed to repeat, with a pit in my throat. "So, you don't feel like you matter to me anymore? You feel like I needed your family as a sort of surrogate safe space more than I needed you?"

We had to mirror the words, taste them. We had to place ourselves in the other's experience from within, in a way that felt harder to access in adulthood without the stink beetles and moths and humming streetlights. Now that there were babies and men and dreams crashing into us, we needed quiet and intention and a new approach to protecting the memory of each other's child selves.

I had been mostly relying on texts to maintain our relationship. I had been sending blocks of tiny texts to maintain something that was built on the ground, in the grass and mud and snow.

And that needed to stop. I needed to start picking up the phone or, better yet, we needed to look at each other. We learned that without that physical presence of voice, touch, eyes, our words were being lost.

It's so easy to add meaning, to distort things based on our moods, our traumas and past unrepaired conflicts. Our two-day deep dive was not a one-time fix. We went on to fail miserably over and over again, but now we had something to fall back on, a reset button to press, a way to ground in a simple technique: pick up the phone or get on a plane and repeat after each other.

It was in the bathroom at the Winnipeg airport after our weekend of work/training and connection that I realized something quite sobering. Quite possibly, Tessa and I were the only ones in the world who knew about this relationship-saving work. I loved that she and I could forever rely on the undeniable science of communication we had learned that weekend. However, if it was just us in the bubble of knowing, that meant Raine was on the outside of it.

I realized I was at the beginning of the greatest mission of my life: doing the work. Now to get Raine on the train that had already left the station, the train whipping past my childhood neighbourhood, approaching the rest of my life at high speeds.

IT'S NOT ABOUT PERFECTION

"When's the last time you eye-gazed for more than thirty seconds?" Dr. John asked from his newly constructed chair in our Sebastopol County Airbnb. Between two thriving, busy and often travelling careers and three kids at different stages, I couldn't remember the last time Raine and I just looked at each other, just intentionally connected. Looks were made in between things, on the way to things. Looks were made in connection to a request or demand or to confirm planning, pick up or drop off. We hadn't just surrendered in the presence of each other for years at this point.

"Let's do it now." I turned toward Raine in response to Dr. John's suggestion. I felt instantly overwhelmed by the arrival of my little self. It was as if she was seated in my lap, grinning and unsure and searching Raine's face for signs of safety, signs of approval. Raine adjusted his seated position a few times, the microadjustments one makes when they are uncomfortable but trying not to disturb your comfort. Like an exhausted parent shifting with a sleeping infant on their chest, desperate not to wake them.

Then he wiped his eyes with the back of his hand. I have, of course, seen him emotional many times, but he always lands in this solid place. He is this strong, capable pillar. I can easily visit his childhood and find the origins of this strength in him, so at times the arrival of his softness, when unexpected, can just gut me. "What is it?" I asked him, in response to the look on his face and the wetness of his sleeve. "I'm just thinking of when we first met," he said.

> "I WAS TERRIFIED THAT WE WERE LOSING EACH OTHER."

At the start of this weekend, I was terrified that we were losing each other. That we perhaps had already lost each other. Then within moments of intentionally connecting in this way, I felt like we were back in the room together. There is no quick fix, but in a simple two-minute eye gaze, I felt like I was really seeing my Raine for the first time in years.

There are so many reasons that coaching is valuable, but I wondered in this moment if the most essential part of the whole thing is the slowing down, the focusing, the space created for nothing but each other and stillness. I felt a renewed curiosity toward him—a profound desire to know everything about him, to have him retell me stories about himself, to open up and invite me into the dark corners of his heart and mind.

A KITCHEN REMODELLED

I was a busy kid. Growing up on the west side of Toronto, in Etobicoke, my early memories are all in motion, images blurred together from the perspective of my BMX bike. I drove that thing everywhere and anywhere. I abandoned it at the bike rack outside of the school, then spent my days fantasizing about riding it home.

I was always looking for adventure with my neighbourhood friends and younger brother, Danny. We owned our neighbourhood. We were like a little gang of kids who ruled the trails, the parks and streets. In winter, we played street hockey when the snow was too high and too deep to make biking a possibility. These early years were full of cuts and bruises, broken bones worn like badges of honour. Missed dinners, neighbourhood fights and good trouble freckled my childhood.

Those years felt like a beautiful distraction from the seriousness of life, an enclosed ecosystem where nothing mattered but our little group and the air pressure in the tires. As adults, we know children should be in wonderment as long as possible, and I lived there immersed in it for my elementary years.

> WE KNOW CHILDREN SHOULD BE IN WONDERMENT AS LONG AS POSSIBLE.

Unfortunately, all good things must end. In the summer after I turned thirteen, my parents sat my brother and I down at our kitchen table. This was not a thing our family did. We weren't the kind to have kitchen-table talks or family meetings, so I immediately prepared for something serious or, at the very least, out of the ordinary.

The anticipation lasted longer than the actual meeting. My parents stood in front of us, somehow taller than they actually were. They very quickly informed us that they were getting a divorce.

My heart dropped through the white-tiled floor, a free fall as if cut loose at the top of an elevator shaft. I remember the smell of the wood from the kitchen table as I rested my head in my hands on its surface. I'd never noticed its smell before.

Our kitchen had recently been remodelled. It was relatively small, but suddenly the walls seemed to be right up against my body. I don't remember what was said after they broke the news. They could have recited *Moby Dick*; I heard nothing but the inside of my own head, the sound like the inside of a shell pressed against your ear, the ocean.

I looked across the table at my brother. He was only ten years old, so naturally I felt the need to protect him, but I was too numb to physically reach out. I wasn't exactly sure what to do in this moment. So with my body tingling I gave him a small reassuring smile that tried to insinuate we'd be okay. I moved my pain over just enough to tend to his, a risky skill to get good at.

As sad as the news was for us, it was equally confusing. I'd never really seen my parents fight. They had arguments over silly stuff, but nothing that would have made me think their marriage was in trouble, nothing that would have made me even consider their marriage as a thing that had the ability to end.

My parents were the cool parents. My mom was active and beautiful. She looks like British supermodel Twiggy, with cute blond hair and big brown eyes. She was always a runner and tennis player. She could throw a football or baseball just as good as any one of our friends.

She had an independent spirit and confidence that undoubtedly shaped what I would seek in a partner. Beauty, brains and distinction. My mom's mom, my grandmother, was tough, she was a fighter. She served in World War Two with the British Auxiliary Air Force. Born in Manchester, England, she lived the last sixty years of her life in Canada in a small but impeccably decorated apartment in Etobicoke. I remember watching hockey with her as a kid. She loved the fights. I admired her resilience and my mom had it as well.

My mom was a great athlete, and she taught me how to compete at an early age. It seems to run in the family. Her sister Sue was a runner, and her younger sister Barb represented Team Canada at the 1976 Olympics in Montreal on the equestrian team. She never let me win at anything; I still have never beaten her at tennis. She believed in my dreams before I had the nerve to say them out loud. When I chased music into every grungy club and half-lit stage around Toronto, she was at every single one, sitting in rooms that smelled like spilled beer. Besides broken PA systems, she clapped the loudest and stayed until the end. She never made me feel like it was a sacrifice. Her love didn't come with conditions, and she never heaped undeserved praise on me. It just came, steady and sure, the same way she moved through everything life handed her. I can't tell you how many times I jumped off the stage at Lee's Palace right after the last note to walk her out to her car to make sure she got out of that Green P lot safely. Growing up in the orbit of a woman like that, self-sufficient, unbreakable, quietly ferocious, leaves a mark that takes a lifetime to fully appreciate.

She had me when she was only nineteen, so I always thought she was hipper than the other moms and we had a lot of fun together. My dad is also a runner. He had to buy a glue gun for the soles of his Brooks running shoes. He used it to fill in the worn-out sections from the countless miles he put in each week.

I loved it when my dad heated up that gun and worked on his shoes. Still now, there's something about the smell of melting rubber that represents to me a type of discipline and work ethic. To this day my dad, at age seventy-eight, runs up to ten miles a week. He still wears Brooks, the bottoms of his shoes still wear out in all the same places, and I still feel comforted when I smell that particular scent of hot glue.

My dad worked hard. His family immigrated from Italy to Canada when he was eight, and he had nothing but the clothes on his back and a willingness to outwork everyone in the room. He never really stopped. He grew up in a modest house downtown, where the bottom floor served as a small grocery store and the upstairs was where he lived with his parents and four siblings. By the time most kids his age were figuring out what to do with their lives, he was already building things. First a business, then a reputation, then whole neighbourhoods from the ground up. Self-taught and self-made, he understood hard work, and that mantra sticks with him today. He started a small construction company when we were kids, and it wasn't uncommon for him to be on the sites seven days a week. He's addicted to learning and hasn't stopped to this day. He's probably bought, read, underlined and highlighted excerpts from hundreds of self-help books.

Looking back, it's easy to see that being married so young was their greatest challenge. They didn't have the emotional IQ or communication skills to help them navigate a family at such a young age. Mix that with the run-of-the-mill stresses of life, and it's amazing they lasted as long as they did.

I keep a picture of my mom and dad from when they were together on my bathroom counter. It's a beautiful, framed photo of them snapped at my aunt's wedding. I look at it every day. I know they still love each other, and the picture is a reminder of how volatile love and life is. I think they fought for their relationship for a time, but ultimately couldn't keep it together.

The Dylan Thomas poem about "not going gently into the night" emanates from that photo. When I see them young and happy—in love—I'm inspired to fight for love, to fight for a relationship that I know they wanted for themselves. I see the value of doing the work. Because of my father's influence, I've never been scared of hard work.

Years later, that picture of my parents doesn't make me sad. It offers me resolve. It gives me purpose and meaning. What my parents had was real. What most couples have is real, at some point. I find comfort in that. Love is real and profoundly beautiful—mostly. I see that picture as just that, a snapshot of the purity of love. The simplicity of it. I smile at my parents, perched beside my toothbrush, as I listen to our boys getting ready for school in pursuit of their own cuts and bruises and good trouble. I listen to them laugh and argue and I wonder how they'll talk about me in therapy in fifteen years. How they will see our marriage and the ways in which our issues become the issues they have to dissect in their future relationships.

BOARDING SCHOOL

The logistics of divorce started almost immediately after the kitchen conversation, taking shape at a speed that felt impossible to catch up to. Now, as an adult, I can recognize that it probably didn't feel fast to them. I am sure there were days or months of private conversations that happened before we, as children, were invited into the reality we didn't know we had been living in.

Not long after my parents split up, they decided it might be a good idea for my brother Danny to go to a private boarding school. I imagine it was meant to be a safety net, an additional structure in the face of such an uprooting shift at home. The loudest and most noticeable shift for me and Danny was the sudden increase in being on our own. While we were already independent neighbourhood explorers, the additional freedom felt unmanageably vast.

Until that point, it was us defining our independence, and then suddenly it wasn't. My mom started working and my dad wasn't able to work less to parent more, so they figured an environment that paid closer attention could be good for Danny, who was just ten at the time.

The school they were looking at was Ridley College in St. Catharines, Ontario. It was only a ninety-minute drive from Toronto, so it wasn't as if they were sending their kid halfway around the world. I was invited to go along for the drive, oblivious to anything more than the fact that I could skip school for the day.

More than skipping school, it was an opportunity for us to be together as a family for the first time in a while, and that felt good. The car ride could have been to anywhere, to do anything. If our car's four seats had us in them, I'd be happy.

We turned off the main exit to St. Catharines, and within minutes crossed a bridge that led to these enormous black gates that greeted us like we'd entered some ancient world. We continued up the longest, straightest driveway I'd ever seen, which finally came to an end at a giant circle, a driveway surrounded by perfectly manicured grass and that finished with a mammoth red brick wall which towered over us. This wasn't a school, but a time machine. I'd only learn about places like this later in movies like *Dead Poets Society* and *Scent of a Woman*.

I had just finished eight years at our local Catholic school, All Saints, where most of our classes were in portables. Our one field didn't have much grass, or a crew to maintain what little there was. If someone didn't bring a soccer ball with them, recess was a drag because the school didn't really have funding for things outside of academics. We never had team uniforms or coaches or a music room.

It was hard not to be impressed with Ridley. We met with a bunch of teachers, the headmaster and some students. Everyone seemed nice and it was obvious my parents were excited by the prospect of Danny going there. I could tell they felt Danny would be safe at this place.

The drive home was quiet but comfortable, familial. With my parents shared excitement about the school, it was easy to imagine, on the hour drive home, that perhaps the divorce had been a temporary blip and we had returned to normal, as if maybe all of this was some terrible joke and my dad was about to prop his elbow on his headrest and toss a "gotcha" to me and Danny in the back.

Bad joke, Dad.

The feeling of back to normal was a mirage. When we got home my parents took me aside and asked if I'd like to join Danny at Ridley. I wondered if the plan had always been to send me too, or if this was really as spontaneous an idea as they were framing it. They explained how important they thought this was for him, but how it might be easier if Danny had his older brother there as well.

I had been excited to start high school with all my friends. But similar to when my parents told us they were splitting up, I felt a calling to show up for Danny, an urgent need to protect my brother. I agreed to go.

"I FELT A CALLING TO SHOW UP FOR DANNY, AN URGENT NEED TO PROTECT MY BROTHER. I AGREED TO GO."

The irony is that Danny was more resilient than me. He was a tough kid, even at ten. I first learned just how tough he was a couple summers prior, when riding our BMXs through a trail we'd built near the creek in our neighbourhood. One day Danny went flying through the air over his handlebars. He must have been going thirty miles an hour when he hit the jump, and landed face-first on a gravel patch, where he then continued to slide ten metres on his chest and stomach. Mom had always pleaded with him to be extra careful, but Danny was uninterested in her warnings—and on this day, he had hit those trails without a shirt on.

When he stood up from this epic fall, his entire chest and stomach were the brightest red any of us had ever seen. Several layers of his skin were left on the gravel stretch.

Our friends almost passed out as Danny stood up. An older next-door neighbour heard the commotion and rushed over, bursting into a panic when he caught sight of my brother.

But there was Danny, tears in his eyes, calmly walking back home. My mom screamed like she'd seen a ghost when he walked in. The entire neighbourhood must have heard her.

As the older brother, I'm not ashamed to say I often looked up to my little brother. He came into the world as if he owned it. He was better than I was at most things and a natural athlete, the kind who makes it look effortless while you're over there grinding to keep up. Wild in the best sense, impossible to contain. It was hard not to admire his fearlessness, his unwavering independent spirit, and I always looked for his opinion on the new OLP. Still do. Danny's a tough customer. I've come to terms with the fact that, in his mind, we'll never outdo Naveed. I love him for that.

My brother endured a lot growing up, mostly because he did things his way. Danny was never one for convention, and Ridley couldn't curb that wildness in him. I'm sure some of his rebelliousness at this new school was a direct result of the divorce. A psychiatrist would probably tell us it was a cry for help, or even an attempt to create a situation that would bring our parents back together. I'm sure some of that might have been true, but some of it was just Danny being Danny.

Ridley was strict, and their tolerance for insubordination was close to zero. Three months in, Danny was out. Now there I was stuck at a boarding school I'd never wanted to go to in the first place, without my brother and without any type of normal life to return back home to in Toronto. The weight of these changes and circumstances suddenly felt like a dark cloud that had replaced any chance of fitting in at school. I missed my brother. I missed my parents being together. Every security I'd had the year prior had vanished.

On more nights than one, I would pack a small bag and encourage myself, *Do it, sneak out the window, climb over those gates and hitchhike back to Toronto*. When the lights went out, I'd lie awake in the darkness and mull over the unwise fantasy.

The dorms were small, so personal items were few. I'd brought my box of CDs with me from home when my dad first dropped me off. It had been sitting untouched under my bed until I finally borrowed some batteries for my Sony Walkman, and U2, Neil Young, Bruce Springsteen and Peter Gabriel started to accompany me through those lonely nights.

Something was different, though. No longer were these albums background music as we swam in our pool during the summer. These songs weren't the soundtrack to the early morning drives in my cousin Nick's old Toyota pickup truck. There was no Nick bobbing his head as we crawled through traffic on the way to the construction sites. These albums—*The Unforgettable Fire*, *Nebraska*, *Harvest*—became my escape. They became my religion. My connection to the words, the chords and the colours mirrored back my struggles and pain. My relationship with music changed. I knew these songs, but now, they knew me.

I found healing in between the notes. The songs became critical to my survival in a way that makes it hard to imagine the person I would have become without that simple box of CDs. I probably wouldn't have chosen music as a career if it hadn't been for that string of events, starting with my parents' divorce, to my leaving home to protect my brother, to my brother's expulsion leaving me alone.

I can also see how, many years later, my inspiration for writing songs is intrinsically linked to that pain. Even now, I summon the fourteen-year-old boy I was then to justify writing. I see him staring up at a blank ceiling in a strange town in a strange building. If the emotional trigger isn't as clear and tangible as those nights in that dorm, writing typically doesn't have the same resonance. For me, music is and will always be a way to express a true experience, a memory or event that can only be fully digested once exposed to the light, like a rust-red frame of film.

I've always said I don't think I've ever written a song when happy. The big question I've always asked myself, the question that haunts me to this day is, Would I erase the pain in my childhood, knowing that I probably would not have developed as profound a relationship with music or pursued a career as an artist? I may never answer this.

OUR FIRST HOME

My dad built our first house *with his bare hands*, a phrase he liked to repeat when he felt we were being ungrateful. I think it must have been a family affair, with enlisted uncles and cousins laying the foundation and building our family's first little dream house in Oakdale.

I can imagine my father's pride and the high stakes of it all, having only been in an apartment in St. James with my mom and two older brothers prior to embarking on the journey of being a homeowner and builder. My father had been raised in an old farmhouse along the highway in Lockport, a modest life he was committed to changing for generations to come.

The house he *built with his bare hands* was huge. A big wooden deck surrounded a rectangular pool with a long bright-blue slide and a hot tub.

My dad owned a pool company, and I would count down the days between summers. Summer in Winnipeg ended too soon. Even as a child, when time feels sort of endless and days last forever, summer still felt like a blip. All too soon the guys would come to winterize the pool at the season's end, and my heart would break.

Looking out in the wintertime in the backyard, the snow would cover everything like a giant cloud, everything but the handles of the ladder, the blue acrylic slide, and the white diving board, which appeared near yellow against the undisturbed white snow. These glimpses of the summer stood as little reminders, promising eventual warmth.

✿

We must have been the first family on our street, because some of my first memories include the not-so-gentle hum of power tools from across the street. Twelve houses would eventually freckle the otherwise empty slice of prairie land.

Along with the new houses came new families—new kids. The two-storey house on the corner with the red shingles and porch swing came with Michael, a kid with fire-red hair who became fast friends with my brother.

One time Michael used the F-word at the table during a family dinner at our house. My dad asked him to leave and never come back. He didn't rage, he just calmly told him to get out and never return. That was Michael's last time at our dinner table.

Now my kids cuss like sailors, and frankly so do I. Somebody somewhere once said, "Never trust anyone who doesn't swear." I kind of believe that.

> "NEVER TRUST ANYONE WHO DOESN'T SWEAR."

At some point a whole new group of families finished building houses or buying spec houses on our street. They seemed to arrive all at once. The women and girls all wore skirts or dresses, and had black hair covers on their heads like babushkas with bobby pins in them. I thought it was so wonderful when all sorts of children were moving into the neighbourhood, although it was quickly revealed that they saw me as a thing to keep on the outside of their plans.

There was one girl next door; her name was Shell. She was a little younger than me, and I thought she was so cool. I was told by Shell, who seemed to offer me slightly more access and insight into their way of life, that I could play with them outside but that they couldn't come into my house, and I couldn't go into theirs because we didn't go to the same church and I didn't attend their *meetings*.

I handed out a birthday party invitation to all the neighbourhood kids one year. My birthday is May 18 and I was so excited; it was spring and warm, and we were playing outside. It felt like an opportune moment to break up all the strangeness, like maybe this was the moment when the children would finally accept me.

One by one they all brought back their invites and said that they weren't allowed to come. I went across the street to the back door of one of the family's homes. The mom had large bug eyes and never blinked. She answered the door and didn't invite me in. I asked her, "Why aren't all the kids allowed to come?" She answered like the response was just sitting in the barrel waiting to be released: "We don't go into the houses of people like you. People who don't attend the same church."

I still do not know what church it was. I just remember the rejection and sadness, the fallen hopes. I thought we all were a community, but somehow I had been born as something they couldn't be a part of. Who their grandparents and parents were before them defined who they were, and years before I was born, it was determined that I couldn't be a part of it.

My friend Cheryl was at the end of my street on the Oakdale side. I loved her so much, but I think her dad hated me. When I managed to get her on the phone to extend an invite to something, she would offer an excited, whispered, "yes"—then call back and cancel.

One time she told me she could have me over. I ran out of my house and up the street as quickly as I could, not wanting to leave time for her to call back and cancel. I went to her back door and ran straight down to the basement into the room we would play in. It was dark. I heard her dad, who I was scared shitless of, yell, “Who’s there? Cheryl?”

I took a deep breath and hid in the closet for what seemed like hours. I listened to him wander around the basement, watching as the light dipped in and out of the slats in the closet door as his shadow passed in front of it. I can’t remember how it ended, which means it was either very traumatizing or entirely inconsequential. I was so frightened of him. Maybe I saw him get after his kids or wife at some point.

PIANO AS A TIGER

The layout of the Charleswood house was key to how everything unfolded. The front door was accented with bevelled glass so high that the image of the arriving guest would warp. We had a doorbell that chimed the brilliant Orthodox Church hook, *ding dong ding dong* . . . and back up . . . *ding dong ding dong.*

As soon as you walked into the house, there was wallpaper to your left, this textured, retro velvet that I would kill to pop in a bathroom today; it would probably be way too expensive now. The entrance acted like it was a big grand hall, but it wasn't really. To your right, was a pillar painted white with a clunky coat stand, and then, boom, there was a step down into the living room and there it was, the upright piano.

This was where it all unfolded. My brain. My hands. My ears. My life. It all came together in that very spot. No matter how many defining memories I may draw from my home and upbringing, the person I am was made at that piano in the sunken living room at 18 Westlund Way in Charleswood.

I am in a conversation with this strange spirit that is one of the most important and wild-beast objects ever created: the piano. It is a tiger to tame. You must approach it with compassion, sink into the thrilling and intimate conversation with the god of music itself. It's incredible, otherworldly, disembodied, an animal to dance with and eventually ride. The piano can be a vehicle, a mode of transportation to anywhere you can imagine.

The piano is my hero, my knight in shining armour, my sanctuary, the place that became a funnel for the angst from my childhood and teenage years. Now, as an adult woman, I feel like I got a pass, all the things I didn't have to do or be because of the protective body of the piano.

Sometimes I go out on stage, and I feel like a bit of a monkey in a cage, restricted to my confined surroundings. I have become good at fighting that feeling in order to land in the present, perform the song and hone the audience, to make them laugh, give them permission to cry. I cannot imagine I would have lasted at all if I had found a voice to sing but not the piano to play.

As a toddler, I would watch TV in the even further sunken-down family room, ingesting the theme songs like they were being played specifically for me. I watched *Sesame Street* and *The Electric Company* and when any new song played, I would run back and forth from the TV room to the piano, playing back what I heard perfectly. If anyone came over, my mom would ask our guests what song they loved. If it was on the radio, chances are I knew of it and I could play it for them. This all fascinates me now, how my skills filled a gap in our household that is now filled by smartphones and Spotify.

To the right of the piano was a step up to the dining room, turn to your right and go down some steps and you're on a landing. Turn left and you go down the stairs to the laundry and low-freezer dungeon. If my mom asked me to go get bread or meat from the low freezer I ran as fast as I could because monsters, obviously.

There was a spare room downstairs that eventually became my eldest brother's room. That's where I would sneak in when he was out, and play his records by Bryan Adams and the Police. I would sing along with a hairbrush in the mirror and envision my future.

As kids, me and my siblings were put on the *practise, practise, practise* train early on. My parents had us studying the conservatory music program for piano. I would eventually study voice with Andrea Labelle in the gifted-youth program at the University of Manitoba.

I would sit on the step down into the living room, watching my brothers practise, watching my mother's patience thin, one foot up on the bench, one hand clenching a wooden spoon, insisting they stay at that piano. By the time I got to go for lessons like them, I treated it like it was the most precious opportunity in the world.

My mom would tuck a cheque into my notebook and send me off to piano. I would habitually check the book to make sure the little rectangular handwritten slip was pressed into my book against the staff paper.

You don't really stop to think about how much your parents spent on you as a kid. The price tag doesn't slap you in the face until you yourself are a parent, or at least old enough to recognize how expensive your dreams can be.

My dad worked so hard. He was always stressed. As kids, you don't know why your parents are so triggered—they aren't individuals yet, they exist only as what they are to you. Now I imagine the sacrifices that had to be made to put a cheque in that book every month.

Children don't yet have the capacity or life experience to understand, never mind take on the suffering and plights of the adults around them, nor should they. I know this, yet still find myself constantly trying to teach my kids some kind of lesson about what it means to work for everything, what kinds of sacrifices are made to provide them with a good life. I am my father all over again, telling them they don't know the value of a dollar. I partly just want them to enjoy it all and not have a care in the world. Isn't that what childhood is about?

GIFTS

Christmas is so loaded with feelings and expectations, met and unmet, sprinkled with invisible landmines you don't uncover for years. When I think of Christmas, it's a combination of magic and worry. We always hosted our relatives including an aunt who had a mood disorder and could be very sensitive around the holidays. She kept Christmases unpredictable.

In the end the music was the best part. I always sat at the piano and played all of the Christmas carols. My mom had music books filled with the lists of holiday songs and the newspapers were saved each year with the titles and notations for the songs of the season. It brought me a lot of joy to make my own holiday album a few years back called Christmas is a Way of Life My Dear.

When my parents had a gnarly quarrel, I would go with my mom to stay at Grandmother's for a few nights. It made me so sad to leave my house, my father and my brothers. One time she didn't have a car for some reason, and we stood freezing in the winter at the bus stop on Kenaston Boulevard. My dad must have driven around for a while before finding us, demanding we get in the car. They must have made up fast or maybe it was just that cold. Extreme temperatures can force speedy treaties, lest you lose a pinky in minus-forty temperatures on a Winnipeg street corner.

I was the youngest, and so I guess the most vulnerable in my parents' eyes, so for some reason they would get into it as to whether I would go with my mom or stay put which made me uncomfortable. I was sure my brothers could hear them talking about who I would stay with. That invoked something in me. Did they have questions? Were they worried? Scared? Hurt that they didn't hear their names in the intense exchanges?

Later in life I learned that it is so important to tell your kids that everything is going to be okay. At a certain point I realized that my middle brother, who has suffered a lot in his life, needed to hear that. I imagined him in his room in his bed, over and over again, listening to our parents screaming. I imagined him hearing my mother leave. I imagine his little heart. He was five years older than me, but we were all innocent kids. It's not easy hearing your parents argue in the first place.

When Raine and I were first together, before we had any help with our marriage, he would cut me off for a few days at a time, not speaking to me while sorting his feelings. I would spend the time in silence, just wishing he would say that everything would be okay.

As a child if I would have a fight with a friend, I would get so panicked. I just wanted to cut to the part where we made up. I wanted to know that everything would be okay. Upon entering my coaching journey, Raine and I both learned that we have to tell each other that yes, we're upset, yes, we need time, even name how much time. But a key part of this agreement is telling each other the words, "But I love you and everything is going to be okay." Even now, those words feel like a warm orange light leaking out of a kitchen window from a house on the horizon. Yes, you are in a blizzard. No, you don't have the appropriate gear to stay alive in subzero temperatures, but there's the house in the distance and you will get to it. You will survive this.

My parents are still together, and although they have gone through a lot together, as all married couples do, they have a very romantic relationship. My father always brings my mother flowers, and they are in a constant practice of giving each other beautiful gifts and cards. I think because Raine didn't see his parents doing that, he hasn't put much of a value on gift-giving. For me, as a child, I observed gift-giving as this thing that has the power to overcome any fight; it was the great equalizer.

We're all so imperceptibly padded with invisible expectations and issues that we can't proactively unearth. There are so many things that just have to come up naturally before you can discover that you are misaligned—before you discover that the thing you thought was a universal truth was merely a product of your particular history, your particular childhood, not a product of all histories and all childhoods.

Often bad gift-givers are also bad gift-receivers. Unless Raine has directly requested an item, he will clearly request that I return the thing. One time I got him a T-shirt in Hawaii when he wasn't with me. He said, "Why would you ever do that?" and asked me to take it back. "I can't take it back, Raine. The cost to ship it back would be worth more than the T-shirt." I think when my parents gave each other gifts, it brought me so much joy as a child because it meant that we were happy in that moment. It meant that they were at peace in their marriage. I can remember how much that meant to me. I can see that that is a place where I identify safety now.

"IT MEANT THAT THEY WERE AT PEACE IN THEIR MARRIAGE."

On days when I don't feel like doing the work, when I don't feel like excavating the very depths of my childhood to understand my patterns and early programming, I wish Raine would just buy me all sorts of useless shit. Bracelets, watches, rings and earrings. Just a whole bunch of crap. I want him to bring me wrapped boxes of stupid shit with beautiful bows on them, symbols of our wellness. And roses. I want constant roses. At times, in the absence of gifts from Raine, I have had actual breakdowns.

As is the case with most things, the thing is rarely the thing. Like that Oscar Wilde quote, "Everything is about sex, except sex."

I remember the potent smell of the roses dying in my childhood kitchen. I loved it, because they were from my dad. They were roses that weren't roses. They were roses that were proof. Proof of wellness. Proof of love and peace. Once the roses were thrown out, it was like hitting the reset button. Everything between the gifts was a minefield.

Now that my father is older, he is sort of quiet. I think this tends to happen, a synchronized softening. Softening of the body creates a softening of the spirit. Now he is a man of few words and more of them are kind than not, resolution based, sweet and sincere. He has become this empath. Perhaps he always was. My parents are still very gift giving and generous, sentimental souls. It moves me now more than ever to receive a thoughtful gift from them. It's our nature to give and receive.

BROTHERHOOD

When I think about my brothers, the memories come at me all at once, hard and fast and tangled up. These memories arrive in a wave of images with floating words that hint of the context. They race through my mind in no particular order, though in most of the memories I am in a fleece nightie. I had a collection of them, these droopy oversized tubes of fleece with long sleeves and a loop of frill around the neck. I believe it was fun Aunt Verna, sister of my mother, who gave me several over the years, wrapped sweetly under the twinkling Christmas tree.

Or maybe it was my maternal grandmother, Isobel. She lived in a retirement community for the last ten years of her life, and remained the self-designated cook for the lot of them until she died. She was epic and social, someone like no one.

Her mother, Alice, was a survivor of the Elkhorn Residential School in Manitoba, maybe a half hour from where I grew up in Winnipeg. My great-grandmother left that place blind and deaf. Despite her plight, she went on to marry and have my grandmother and several other children.

She taught them to be hard-working people with a value for education and being proper.

My great-grandmother knew everything "British style": how to make a bed, hold your fork, place a tablecloth. She knew how to knit and sew and crochet. My great-grandmother showed my grandmother, and my grandmother showed me. I knit all the time. I feel the matriarchs of my family in my hands as I loop the yarn around the needle in repetition.

Alice is this beautiful length of thread, leading me to my Indigenous roots. From her we have Verna, my very handsome Uncle Johnny, and Uncle Walter. I can imitate the way Walter says, "Hi Channy." As soon as I get on the phone with my Auntie Pat, my voice automatically turns into this full Manitoba-bumpkin Métis sound. Sometimes I am not sure if Raine is horrified or if he finds it endearing that I naturally match them tonally. I match them the way I did as a child, the way I match songs on the radio to tones on a piano. The instinct to sing along is foundational in me.

As the youngest, I know there will come a time when there are no more voices to mimic and mesh with, so I revel in each conversation and the subtle departures my dialect takes in reflection of them.

Michael was always smaller than Trevor, who was very handsome and tall like my dad with the eyes of my grandmother. My father and all his siblings are very tall, as Ukrainians tend to be. Of my father's six sisters and six brothers, the women are all at least five foot ten and clearly look like both parents. It's hard to say who my dad resembles more.

Despite my brothers' size difference, they were constantly wrestling. My mom would be in the kitchen cooking, or just not really paying attention, as they rolled around the family room, *The Dukes of Hazzard* playing on the small clunky TV while they pinned each other with their forearms and shins.

They would sweat and hold each other in a position for as long as the other could take it. When an arm was about to dislocate, when a finger was about to break, someone would finally say "uncle."

This moment would never come quickly enough for me. My brothers would make a series of desperate, terrible noises that would force me up and off of the piano bench. I somehow knew instinctively when something shifted from fun to dangerous. I would leap in to throw myself in the middle of it. The shift from play to violence happened slowly, little changes in facial expressions as the placement of their noises moved deeper into their bodies and throaty yelps transformed into guttural rumbles. I usually helped the one that I was most nervous for, the one I thought was losing.

I close my eyes and I'm back in my fleece nightie. I can hear myself calling my mom, trying to enlist her power in a moment of things getting bad. If I was lucky, she would leave the kitchen and come over to simply state, "That's enough."

My mom did the meals each night, but my dad cooked a roast on Sundays. My dad's family—his whole clan, as my mom liked to call them—started as Ukrainian Orthodox but at some point became Baptists, bordering on Pentecostal. Hands were raised, spirits were broken, hearts were served up on a platter to Jesus.

There were chapters in my life when I bought into the whole church thing. I had been sent to a private girls' school, where we were educated in a more progressive style, and the kids were from all sorts of backgrounds. I decided that I was born from a family of God, but that they raised a different breed in me.

My brothers didn't go to a private school and had a very different education than I did. Sometimes I just felt so different from my family. Not in a black sheep way, but in the way that I experienced how children in the same family in fact grow up with different versions of the same parents, based on the birth order and gender and your parents' capacity at the time of your birth.

> "SOMETIMES I JUST FELT SO DIFFERENT FROM MY FAMILY."

IN THIS LIFE

The things you are so resentful for can be those that make the best part of you. There is just no question in my mind, that the hardest things I had to face in my life, as a child, teen or otherwise have shaped me to being a curious and compassionate person that feels the pain and suffering of others.

I have never even been regretful of that part of myself or tried to fight it. I go into the fire. I am happy and privileged to be with others upon request in their darkest hours. I am not scared. It's because of the cold and intimidating place I come from found warmth and hope no matter what.

The tough, gritty girl, meets soft essence of me, the lilt and soul of my song within a sad and dark tribute is because I am a quintessentially Canadian girl. There is a personality to the songs we Canadian girls write. We're Kathleen Edwards's "Hockey Skates" meets Anne Murray's "You Needed Me." The Jonies and the Nellys. The list is phenomenal. I always get asked by people, "Is there something in the water?"

> "WE ALL COME FROM TRAUMA."

Canada is a harsh climate, especially for those of us in the coldest provinces and there is a lot to reckon with. The sights we see, our colonial mess. The mosaic makes for something symbiotic. We all come from trauma. Whether it be first generation or in our DNA. Still, we're always trying. We just don't ever give up. I am so grateful for that part of myself.

Mental health is the hottest most vicious fire to go into for me. A family member in mania would scorch me. The rage, the shame, the frustration. But on the other side of mania is a profound meeting with depression. The cycle got ahold of me, as its witness for much of my young life. I felt feelings and connection that can only come from a desire to comfort someone you love who is going through it, their innocence piercing my soul at the end of it all.

I wrote "In This Life" on a guitar one evening in Vancouver when I was supposed to be having a great night in my career, a show with Canadian superstars in aid of Cancer Research. One of my family members had gone missing back in the Peg at the coldest time of year. People get found frozen in Winnipeg, so I feared the worst. True and authentic, unconditional love wrote the song "In This Life."

> Let me tell you who you really are
> you're my comfort, not a superstar
> I can reach up and bring you back down to the ground
> And give you everything you dream about
> You can run from me you can hide from me
> but I am right beside you in this life
> I was not ever meant to get too far

BRING THAT BOY

> I come from a man with a sword in his hand
> I was born of the raging sea
> Shunned by a brother
> Ached for a lover
> Bring that boy to me

My big brother had plans on a cold winter night. But so did my parents, and they needed him to babysit last minute. So the big brother had to babysit the little sister instead of being out in the neighbourhood with his buddies. I can now imagine how much crappier it was to have to babysit me than going out to be with the boys from the neighbourhood. I think boys need to play outside more than anything. More than math or science, they need to compete and conquer. I took that away from him that night. Before my parents could pull out of the driveway, I had already done the bratty little sister thing, and let my parents know, by running outside in my fleece nighty, that big brother was not happy about having to stay home with me.

While my mom checked her lipstick in the visor mirror, my dad came in to clarify with big brother what the expectations were. These days, we helicopter, and we coddle. We overanalyze our responses, and our kids have all sorts of input into how things will flow. I am not sure we have found the correct balance between democracy and dictatorship.

There has to be an adult in the room. It's incredibly difficult to know when you have been too soft and when you have been too hard on your child. Our input is like medicine. Doesn't medicine impact people differently? If I am too involved, then I have smothered. If I give space, I am neglecting. It is impossible to get it right all of the time. I forgive my parents, and I hope my kids one day forgive me. We are all doing our best with the tools we have at the time. I hope we can forgive ourselves. That may be the hardest one of all.

I will never forget how my big brother told me he wanted to be left alone after my father—in his way—clarified the expectations for that night to him before going back out to the car warming up in the driveway, my mother listening to B.J. Thomas or Elvis on eight track as the exhaust plume streamed into the frigid Winnipeg night. It broke my heart. I don't know who we love more, and who matters more, our siblings or our parents sometimes. These relationships are deep and wide, heavy and complex.

We're all so different in our DNA and our presentation, and how we process and remember. We mate and procreate to heal the wounds we aren't even necessarily aware of.

When I met Raine he was soft, kind, strong and collected. He really seemed like he couldn't be rattled but under all of that was a quiet call for healing. I truly believe that we are brought to our person, and they to us, so that we can fix something with them that was wrong, find something that was lost, create something we yearned for in our childhood.

> Now we're on the run
> Shield our babes with his gun
> Teach em my daddy's scream
> Are we cooling the fire
> Or are the flames getting higher
> Bring that boy to me

HISTORY

One of my favourite moments working on our relationship came in an Imago Institute workshop Raine and I attended, when we were told very matter of factly, "We forgive our parents. They did the best they had with the tools they had."

I stopped the instructor and said, "Hang on . . . we do what?" I realize all people have wounds that need to be reconciled with or forgiven. I often arrive at the conclusion that what is stopping so many of us from connection and healing is our private pain and shame. It's fascinating that we now know that trauma is stored in the DNA and even random anxiety can be caused by something from a parent's or grandparent's past traumas or experiences.

My father is my hero because he comes from so much suffering in his history and still, he persevered. My great-grandfather came over to Canada to escape Stalin. My father was raised in a little farmhouse that my great-grandfather acquired on a plot of land that seems harmless in the summer months but is relentlessly cold and cruel in the winter. My Baba and Gigi, as my Ukrainian grandparents were affectionately called, raised my father and his eleven other siblings in that little farmhouse. I grew up going there on the weekends and have such fond memories of the old upright piano in the front room where the Sunday Disney movie would play while the aunts were peeling potatoes for dinner. My baba passed while I was still in my mom's belly. It has always been so sad to me that I didn't get to know her personally.

> "MY FATHER IS MY HERO BECAUSE HE COMES FROM SO MUCH SUFFERING IN HIS HISTORY AND STILL, HE PERSEVERED."

Eventually my great-grandfather Nicholas would take his own life in that farmhouse. His death and the circumstances around it would permeate generations, nearly undetectably, like gas seeping through a crack under a doorway.

Nicholas came over with trauma, and my father's father would have been the recipient of it. My Gigi was quiet as I knew him and as far as I could tell he loved me, loved all of us. He wore suspenders and worked hard and had piercing blue eyes and knew how to love with proper grandparent love. When he took me on the tractor during harvest, I felt so chosen, knowing there were so many other grandchildren to choose from. We would ride through the swaying wheat in the fields, for what felt like miles.

We all do the best we can with the tools we have as partners and parents. No one talks about it, but I am pretty sure that my Gigi liked to drink, surely devastated from his childhood and the untimely loss of his father and his wife, the mother of his twelve children. My dad never really drank at all.

But even recently I have begun to let my dad know that his childhood experience probably wasn't very healthy, and that while it made an ambitious, strong man out of him, the little boy, Johnny, probably had many needs unmet.

To be fully honest with someone you love is incredibly painful. I have endless compassion and praise for my father's achievements and what he overcame in a family of twelve, to grow up in that little farmhouse off the highway—to come from such a trying background. I romanticize some of the life he lived in real time. The farmhouse, the little barns and buildings around the property, the fences and gravel road, the cold heartless quiet blanket of beautiful snow that covered the fields, and the piano I played while people listened and celebrated little me. But was my dad seen and celebrated there as a child? Was he safe from the cold? Were his needs met?

My dad is a handsome, charismatic, generous, proud man, father and husband. He was at every single competition I performed in during my musical development. Every recital and play. He was present, supportive. He was my first love. He provided for his family and became the man no one ever thought he could become, to give us so many things that he never had.

My dad was smart and full of hard-earned skill. He was a carpenter and a plumber. He was an inventor, this tireless, persistent force, bigger than life. But what I also now recognize in him more than anything is a boy given more responsibility than any child should be burdened with.

At times my dad will see me knitting and remind me that he had to finger knit as a child. They didn't have an endless supply of needles; if his mother was knitting, she used the needles, and he used his tiny fingers. She would tell him winter was coming; he better start knitting a scarf if he wanted to be warm. As the second-born, he was a boy expected to act like a man.

I wonder what kind of yarn he worked with. I would give anything to see a photo of him bundled up in the scarf he made himself as a child for his own survival. The walk to school was of course miles long, deathly cold. It's a miracle we're all here. Not until you grow up and get married and have your own children do you see where you have inherited all your tools and traits from. My work ethic is from him and maybe from my baba who was known to have a baby and go out in the fields to pick potatoes the next day.

When we meet our partner, it's like a magical pull, courtesy of nature. But that person is the tip of the iceberg. Once the stresses of children and multi-tasking and day-to-day frustrations come in, we meet the little boy that was our childhood selves, face to face; we see the grief of our fathers and grandfathers, the pain and struggle in our great-grandfathers. Maybe, we even find ourselves running from Stalin.

ST. PIERRE

Finding the right space to be creative is almost as important as the creativity itself. I've learned over the years that it's typically not a comfortable surrounding that helps channel your best.

OLP made two albums on the island of Maui. While it sounds idyllic, I was overcome by the internal turmoil and strife within the band while making the first of those two, *Gravity*. It became apparent during that recording that we were on divergent creative paths with guitarist Mike Turner.

The decision to part ways was not taken lightly, but that fateful conversation between Mike and I on Maui became the impetus to write "Innocent" and "Somewhere Out There." Had we not split with Mike, I may have never written those two songs, and the trajectory of the band would have most certainly been different or compromised.

The few years after that were not easy, but we've remained friends throughout it all. It was a thrill to have Mike join us onstage during some of the shows on the *Spiritual Machines 2* tour.

Healthy in Paranoid Times started on Maui as well, but ended in Malibu fourteen months and six recording studios later. This record turned into an albatross. After thinking we had finished the album about six months in, we rented Studio B at Westlake Audio in Los Angeles. It was the same room where Michael Jackson recorded *Thriller*, but we didn't rent it to record anything. Columbia Records president Donnie Ienner was eager to hear the follow up to the platinum-selling *Gravity*.

This day would go down in OLP history as one of our darkest. As much as Donnie wanted to like what he heard, he left underwhelmed. We left the studio that night lost and frustrated, with no other choice but to go back to the drawing board—new songs, more studios.

In November of 2003 I was sitting in the lounge at Metalworks in Toronto when my cell rang. It was Lisa Zbitnew, president of Sony Music Canada. Lisa was relatively new to the label, but we had a good rapport. I knew within the first thirty seconds of the call something was up. Lisa let me know the budget for *Healthy in Paranoid Times* had surpassed one million dollars. To say this was a shock would be an understatement. That sixth album was destined to have baggage, but the music is still some of my favourite in our catalogue. "Angels/Losing/Sleep" was born out of this frustration.

After we retreated to our respective homes, I woke up one morning and wrote that song while looking out our living-room window into the golden Malibu hills. The song just poured out of me, and I'm convinced that's what happens as stress builds.

I guess with some artists that doom may cause a writer's block, but for me it's simply the ember that eventually sparks something special. I'm at peace with the fact I'm drawn to situations that bite back. Conflict helps me internalize and become reflective, which in turn creates better palettes to write music and lyrics to.

When Chantal and I decided to make a record together, we chose St.-Pierre-et-Miquelon as the place we'd write our first record. There were all the same predispositions I'd endured with OLP. In the summer,

St. Pierre is an enchanting romantic island, a French territory off the south coast of Newfoundland. Cobblestone streets are lined with amazing French bistros and cafés. The pace is slow. People are friendly. Like most Europeans, the people there work to live, and this is reflected strongly in the island culture. So much so that a café we visited for lunch took our order, then proceeded to let us know they were taking their own lunch break. It lasted over an hour, but we had a bottle of wine, some bread and a Scrabble board, so we accepted this change.

This "romantic" atmosphere wasn't going to work for us, so the plan was not to return in the summer, but in the dead of winter when half the population had left for Nice, and the other half stayed inside until spring. I liked the idea of familiarity on St. Pierre, but looked forward to the more challenging winter setting.

We landed there again during a snowstorm on January 20. The wind was as harsh as we'd heard about, and three feet of snow lined the icy roads. It felt more like the Arctic than that quaint fishing town we'd visited in the summer. Our hotel was comfortable enough, but the wind howled through every crack it could find. The island even surprised me in terms of how quickly it made us realize it was going to be our adventure's protagonist.

I brought an old record player and some vinyl to fill the space when we weren't writing. It's important to note that I was hyperaware that we'd agreed earlier, with Dr. John, that this trip was also going to be a chance to reconnect. I tried not to lose sight of that, but quickly noticed something was off. Either through touch, or her words, or a simple glance, Chantal is always looking for connectivity. So, when I started to notice she wasn't prioritizing closeness, I knew something was up.

We were three flights and 3,500 miles away from our young kids, and I felt the stress of that. It was the first time we'd both been away like this, so I wondered if that reality was hitting Chantal harder than it was hitting me.

ST. PIERRE

During a particularly challenging session with Dr. John, he had asked us when we last spent a full day together. We stared at each other on the droopy couch, searching each other's eyes for the memory. Eventually Raine said, "When we were in St. Pierre. We were there for a show, but it was an off-day and we just walked around aimlessly and played Scrabble and drank wine." I remembered it right away. St. Pierre had become a sacred place for us both. In was in St. Pierre that the initial idea of making an album together first bloomed.

It took a little while for this nugget of an idea to turn into an actual living, breathing song, but eventually the moment was right, the mood was perfect, real-life obligations fell aside enough to prioritize making it happen.

The song was called "I Love It When You Make Me Beg." Raine's title. He presented the hook to me, and I thought it was beautiful. The rest of the song unfolded quickly after that, and an album felt inevitable.

Our lives were so busy. By the end of the day, once dinner was made and the dishes were done, all we had energy for was plopping ourselves on the couch or frolicking with the kids. When we had a free window, we would just spend it with the family. Inevitably, this moment, with our love at the very bottom of a giant list of priorities, coincided with our relationship being at an all-time low. I felt distant and disconnected from Raine. It can just sort of happen. Between raising kids and all the chaos of careers and artistic visions, and our independent paths. I yearned for reconnection.

Suddenly it felt essential that we prioritize making this album together, and what better place to do it than in St.-Pierre-et-Miquelon, the origin of the idea.

We decided to bring a film crew with us and turn the trip into a documentary. We didn't know what we were going to find, but our intention was to go deep and explore our personal and creative relationship. We decided to go in the dead of winter, because why not make it as hard as possible on ourselves? Why not encourage the landscape to reveal the darkest parts of ourselves to each other in the isolated solitude of a hotel room away from our beautiful home and children?

St. Pierre is very beautiful in the summer. It's idyllic and charming and peaceful while bubbling with energy and community. The winters, however, are harsh. The majority of people go back to the mainland of France to avoid the unforgiving plummet in temperatures. All the shops and restaurants I was excited to visit again were closed for the winter, and we were left with the howl of the wind in our ears and the dependability of room service.

Our plan was to be vulnerable. To slow down enough, away from the noise of everyday life, to really connect with each other—and, additionally, to invite the audience into the intimacy of being a songwriter, the increased intimacy of doing it with a partner.

I believe we did that. But it was also a dark time, a valley of sorts. I missed our children desperately. They were just too far. It was the first time both Raine and I were away at the same time. There is something about him being with the kids if I am not; it's almost as if I am there, him as my representative. For the snotty noses and tantrums, and the details of disappointments and triumphs on the way home from school, with their dad they are completely covered even if I am away.

I just sunk to a low, and I was weepy and sensitive. To make matters worse, the windy, dark island was like this character that wanted to test us further, like it was trying to come between us. I wish we chose an island off of Tahiti or something. Of course it makes for good music, but a reconnection with my man? Not so much.

However, the experience and subsequent documentary facilitated our first conversations around sharing our coaching journey with our audience and community. If I have learned anything as an artist, it's that none of us are alone. Even the most specific and nuanced experiences are universal when you start sharing them.

I consider it a calling and a purpose to stick my neck out there and be the first to say or try something should it maybe help others. I am not too proud. I am not scared, especially when I feel that call to action. A song is a call to action, an idea is a whisper from the gods.

“EVEN THE MOST SPECIFIC AND NUANCED EXPERIENCES ARE UNIVERSAL WHEN YOU START SHARING THEM.”

OVERWHELMING THE NERVOUS SYSTEM

One of the main tools we've learned from all our work with marriage therapists and couples' coaches are the concepts of self-regulation and coregulation.

To me, being able to monitor and control your own feelings is a superpower. We are nothing if not our feelings; however, allowing our feelings to determine outcomes isn't always smart. Regulating feelings so you're not acting on impulse is key. It's taken me my entire existence to learn this. I operate on feelings.

As a creative being, I lean on feelings to inspire my writing. It's the unregulated feelings that produce the creative juice, so finding a balance where I'm responsibly handling my emotions can be a battle. I often feel like a hypocrite when telling my kids how important it is for them to self-regulate.

The idea of coregulation adds another wrinkle to the creative equation. As much as it may seem hypocritical to say this, the tension in my relationships, especially with Chantal, often becomes the spark for reflection, introspection and, ultimately, writing.

Everything we're taught about relationships is to either self-regulate or coregulate so there's calm and safety in stressful situations. Managing these emotions is a battle that I sometimes choose not to fight.

This, of course, goes against even my better judgment, but I've admitted that I don't think I've ever written a song that's worthwhile when I've been happy.

This was most evident in St. Pierre. Chantal saw that adventure as a disaster. The virtually empty village, the horrible weather, being so far from home and our young kids. My perspective was the complete opposite. The bitter cold island in January was exactly what we needed to create the album.

We tried multiple times to write that record back in Los Angeles. In six years since deciding to begin, we'd written one song. Don't get me wrong, "I Love It When You Make Me Beg" was part of the reason we decided to make an album, but it felt increasingly impossible to find the space to write more. We were pulled in such different directions, there simply wasn't enough focused conflict to draw out good music in Los Angeles, at least for us as a couple. The distractions made it impossible to truly dig into and dissect our relationship, find chords and words and arrangements that would live up to the high expectations we had for our music. As with my solo work, I needed our first full album together to be a collection of works that our kids would respect and get to know their parents through.

> "THE DISTRACTIONS MADE IT IMPOSSIBLE TO TRULY DIG INTO AND DISSECT OUR RELATIONSHIP."

As is evident in the documentary, my struggle with both self-regulation and coregulation is clear. I would never say the conflict was purposeful, but the idea of turning us into this perfect, coregulated couple would have made for some boring-ass music.

Love is messy. Relationships can be messy and still be beautiful. We were adamant about capturing the true nature of our relationship, as it pertained to our creative process. The film is titled *I'm Going to Break Your Heart* for a reason.

One of my favourite songs I've been a part of is "I Can Change," which was captured in its creative entirety in the film. The inception point for this song was a disagreement about an idea Chantal had in our little hotel room. I wasn't feeling inspired by a piano idea she had, and my reaction had very little self-regulation as a loving partner.

At one point she challenges me as to why I was so insensitive, and accuses me of looking down on her idea, like I'd just eaten shit. I denied it—until I saw the unedited takes from the day. But the conflict that ensued led to Chantal writing the opening piano line, and inspired the melodies and the lyrics.

In the documentary you see the song being born, finished and then recorded live as it exists on the album today. As much as I hate to say it, I would have never written the words "I Can Change" had we been sitting around laughing and coregulating.

This isn't to dismiss how critical regulation is as a tool. I still believe that love is messy, and conflict is both normal and healthy. But what I also believe is that the ability to be aware of the need to self-regulate or coregulate more quickly is important. Getting stuck is when it becomes destructive. Writing "I Can Change" was coregulation.

Even Chantal admits how hearing me sing that for the first time immediately healed our earlier conflict.

If nothing else, understanding that having the self-awareness and skills to regulate feelings is vital to a healthy relationship. We need to understand that we can't expect perfection—but progress is important.

EMPATHY

I'm convinced that there's a connection between empaths and creativity. Chantal easily picks up and feels, deeply, the emotional states of those around her. She also hears music in this heightened way. Combine that with her perfect pitch and being classically trained, and you have an artist that can channel some of her favourite artists, people like Carly Simon or Joni Mitchell, Ella Fitzgerald or Billy Joel.

By the time she ended up in the studio with Drake, Chantal had written tons of hit pop songs for the likes of Gwen Stefani, Kelly Clarkson and Josh Groban. To do that, she led with empathy to cater to each individual artist.

There are stark differences between the way we each write and hear music. I rely much more on instinct. I was never trained. As a self-taught musician, I fumble around to find the right chords, melodies and words. It's almost impossible for Chantal to do that. She can't sing a wrong note. She can't play a wrong chord. She knows too much.

I remember the first time I introduced her to the Deftones. What's brilliant about the Deftones is the melodies Chino Moreno sings over the band's complex ninth chords. Some of those melodies can sound slightly out of tune or grind a bit to the human ear. It drove her crazy.

Chantal being highly technical and trained as a musician, while also being an empath, is a bit of an earned cheat code. She can immediately tell what key a song is in. She can play along in real time to a song she's never heard before. It's at once maddening and incredible.

In some ways, the specific differences in our creative approach mirror issues in our relationship.

Being highly sensitive means Chantal feels my moods or words more than others might. That puts me at a deficit immediately, because, as an artist, well—not gonna lie—I have a lot of moods. Especially when I'm writing.

Chantal takes that same technical proficiency she has as a musician and applies it to our relationship. It is science to her on many levels, no different than music theory.

My approach, much like how I write music, is different. It's fascinating to see these contrasts in style play out interpersonally.

I remember noticing these two approaches while watching the initial edits of our documentary. Chantal can appear impatient, because in her brain it's music. Any conflict should be resolved no different than the way she can write a song. Zeroes and ones, as far as how melodies work over chords and what harmonies should be applied. I need time. I need to fumble around. It's much slower for me because I'm looking for the essence of the chord or lyric or harmony. This doesn't work as well in a relationship, but it does hold water for the theory of why opposites attract. The idea of finding that balance between us is key.

"THE IDEA OF FINDING THAT BALANCE BETWEEN US IS KEY."

Chantal will tell you that anytime a song is playing in the house or on the radio her brain has to analyze it. She hates it, but it's simply the way her brain works. That applies to us as well. She has to analyze and dismantle my words or actions any time we have even the smallest conflict. I'm not saying that there isn't value in digging in and figuring out the root causes of conflict, trying to learn how to repair quicker and better. I'm just fascinated by our differences.

I love the science of the brain and how it applies to our happiness. My only beef is being in a constant state of analysis. You can't love the work more than the outcome. Growth, of course, is the product of effort, but it is possible to become paralyzed by over analysis.

There have been many times in my career where I've written a song I'm in love with, but there are a few lingering lyrics that aren't quite right. Reimagining or rewriting those lyrics can be the worst chore ever given to man. I've spent weeks trying to finish a lyric, and the torture can almost turn me against the song altogether.

SHANGRI-LA

Rick Rubin has produced some of the most iconic music of the past three decades. From the Beastie Boys to the Red Hot Chili Peppers to Johnny Cash, there is no question Rick has tapped into something different that artists are drawn to. At the same time, Rick has never been accused of being a hands-on producer—often he is barely in the room when making records.

As an artist, I can see why this approach might not work for everyone, but the first time I walked into his Shangri-La studio in Malibu it all made sense.

After surviving St.-Pierre-et-Miquelon, Chantal and I returned to LA with ten or eleven songs. Just as we needed to leave the comfort of Los Angeles while writing, that experience needed to be honoured when we were actually recording the songs as well. Sure, we'd cut a great live version of "I Can Change" in our hotel room, but the rest of the songs needed a proper studio to help capture their essence. It would have been easy to set up at home. I prided myself on the vintage gear I'd collected over the years to build a world-class home studio. I was always proud to say that you won't find a Ferrari in our driveway, but inside you'll find a vintage 1960s Neve console and every great piece of tube gear and microphones.

On the surface I thought we'd be crazy to go anywhere else to record, considering how difficult St. Pierre was. I knew the thought of going away again would terrify Chantal.

A good friend of ours, Jason Lader, who works with Rick on most of his projects, had just been working up at Shangri-La with the Avett Brothers and Smashing Pumpkins, and let me know there was a couple weeks available in May if we wanted to get in.

This was an easy yes. Shangri-La was not only Rick's private studio, but history runs deep there, as it was opened by the Band and is featured in *The Last Waltz*. To add to this mystique, Rick inherited Bob Dylan's old tour bus, parked it on the grass on the property and converted it to a remote studio. Rumour has it Neil Young loves to get high in that bus and record all his vocals and acoustic guitar tracks there.

What's most impressive about Shangri-La is what you don't see. The studio is repainted before each new artist arrives. The walls are all white, and there's a gorgeous old white Bösendorfer piano that sits quietly alone in one room surrounded by windows. The main living room is expansive, but only houses a large black couch and bean-bag chair.

There isn't one photo of Eric Clapton or Bob Dylan hanging on a wall, and, despite the many millions of records sold by the artists who've recorded there, you won't find a gold record anywhere. No matter who walks in there to make music, the studio is set up to protect their creative intentions. It's safe from any outside influences or insecurities solely because of the attention to detail that Rick and Shangri-La offer.

The vibe fit Chantal and myself perfectly. It was only twenty-five minutes from our home, and we'd just dug deep into the concept of intention. Shangri-La was intentional by design. It came with no baggage. The metaphor of repainting the interior walls was not lost on me as a metaphor of a clean slate. This is exactly what we needed as a couple, especially after the hardships of the island. It was as if Shangri-La knew what our challenge was.

We set some ground rules as to how we would speak to each other, and the type of respect we needed to mirror; after all, we were now bringing in other musicians to play on the album. The dynamic was about to change drastically, and I saw this as a test for me to prove I was listening and, more important, learning from all the work we'd been doing.

I think every relationship hits a point where you look at your partner and you are forced to come to terms with who and what they are. I absolutely believe humans have the capacity to change, but only incrementally. I put it between ten and fifteen percent; that's about the extent of most people's ability and desire to change. In the scope of things, this is dramatic.

Everyone has that realization at some point that your partner is either in it to be better and willing to evolve, break cycles and communicate more honestly; or, they're unwilling or incapable. I was willing, but being willing and actually doing the necessary work to change are vastly different.

If St. Pierre was a low point in our marriage, I needed Shangri-La to be the high point.

After all these years of baby steps, I wanted this experience of recording our album to signify real growth. We'd just written songs about these exact topics, with deeply personal lyrics, and we had written them while making a documentary exposing our failures as a couple.

I knew the burden was on me to prove that "I Can Change" wasn't some bullshit lyric written to appease Chantal in the moment. I knew for the sake of myself, Chantal and our family it was time to put it all into actual practice.

> "I KNEW FOR THE SAKE OF MYSELF, CHANTAL AND OUR FAMILY IT WAS TIME TO PUT IT ALL INTO ACTUAL PRACTICE."

BURN IT DOWN

Partners are, simply put, number one to each other, at the top of the pyramid of life—or they should be—in the science of coupling. Everything and everyone else, is a distant third: the job, the hobbies, the friends, the in-laws, even the kids.

My parents were young and stressed with their own struggles as a married couple. As kids, we would absorb that. If they weren't good, we weren't good. If they didn't have peace, we didn't have peace. Raine and I rarely have big blow-ups and don't make a habit of letting our conflicts play out in front of the kids. Unfortunately, even the best habit management can falter given the wrong set of circumstances.

I woke up and saw a social media post by Raine. A much younger, very beautiful woman—a blue-eyed, raven-haired beauty—was playing the piano and singing one of my husband's songs. The girl is irrelevant to the story. I think she is perfectly lovely. There is no back story of a rivalry or drama, and it's nothing personal. She arrived only as a crack in my feeling of safety in our kingdom walls.

Our work with Dr. John would tell us to pause and set a time to discuss an issue I was having. I would, in theory, calmly tell Raine in a few sentences what was bothering me. Irrational or not, I would try not to judge my feeling and state it calmly, nonjudgmentally, just a nice clean, "Hi my love, so when I saw the post on Instagram this morning I thought at first that it was me there playing the piano and singing and I thought it was so sweet you had posted me, and of course I realized very quickly it was a much younger beautiful *other* woman. My heart sank. Would you be open to taking it down, my love?"

My child self doesn't have those tools; she hadn't been through decades of coaching, and in this moment, on this day, she felt replaced, unchosen and unprotected. I thought, "But *I'm* Raine's piano-playing/singing queen." It was almost as if I was momentarily putting my entire value to him on the thing I do. Our careers and skills have never been at the centre of our connection, but here I was feeling like, "Wait, I am the only one allowed to play his songs. There can be no other piano-playing brunette beauty in this kingdom."

Fear does snaky things.

In a world in which I was able to express the feeling at my highest frequency, at my most calm, and clear, Raine's reaction to my vulnerability would have then been to repeat back to me what I told him, almost exactly if possible, and then of course he would perform his only duty: protecting my feelings by taking down the damn post.

Sadly, this is not what happened. Instead, I went absolutely crazy. I essentially burned down the castle. I called his mother, our friends and lost my shit like never before.

It was a Sunday, and Raine was on the couch with the boys watching the football game in zombie mode. I entered the room like a prowling lion.

I don't know that I have ever lost it on Raine in front of the kids like this. *NFL Sunday* could only partially drown out my ferocity. I needed everyone enrolled in my cause, including our children. I needed the collective to say, "Yeah, what the hell is he thinking?" I wanted everyone to agree with me that Raine had absolutely lost his mind and done the most terrible evil thing; that men are stupid; and that now Raine was just another one of those typical men and that I was a full victim. The subconscious goal in seeking safety was to pile everyone on and turn everyone in the entire kingdom against Raine. Safety in numbers perhaps.

Off with his head.

Eventually, the entire village was on fire, and my behaviour outdid Raine's original *crime* of posting someone covering his hit song. Eventually we needed some emergency repair work, and I got to learn, for the ten-thousandth time, that it's not so much what happens to you, it's how you process it.

Sometimes it starts with one thing and then the grievances start airing—and then the next thing you know voices are raising and all the labelling is on like Donkey Kong and words are ripping through the house like wildfire and you've thrown the kitchen sink at the topic and now you're both these awful demons . . .

Once the issue has spiralled beyond recognition, it can be hard to remember what the inciting incident was. Someone was late? Someone forgot to pick up the kids or call a father-in-law or clean out the car? Someone added too much garlic to the Caesar dressing? How could something so small lead to, "I have had it!" Or "I'm done." Or the worst one, "You *always* do this . . ."

Raine and I have had an ongoing rule for nearly thirty years: no name-calling or cussing each other out, even when conflicts arise. We are very good at this rule, until the moments we aren't. Though those moments are few and far between, they leave marks that need to be tended to, loved up, healed.

There are so many reasons this rule can falter. We are imperfect, we fall victim to the moment, and can easily spiral and become the most terrible version of ourselves. This can happen loudly in relationships where you feel safe, where you aren't constantly censoring yourself for fear of being left.

> “WE VILLAINIZE OUR PARTNERS AT TIMES.”

We villainize our partners at times. They become the enemy as we make up stories and assign motives to each other that simply aren't true. We are all storytellers, after all.

From the moment we are born, we scream bloody murder. Our story in the form of tears is so compelling that milk suddenly releases from a mother's breast. Storytelling is our first talent. All of us. It's paramount to our survival. And if we're not telling our wild stories out loud, we're telling them to ourselves.

It is imperative to have a plan, and put that plan into practice for when those fires start crackling.

CPR is a lifesaving tool in more places than just the side of a pool. Dr. John taught us it can stand for "catch, pause, repair." I find the *catch* part easy. Raine doesn't want me to pick every battle. It's too much. Little heartbreaks can happen twenty-five times a day, and to fight twenty-five battles a day is exhausting and unsustainable. The *pausing* part has never been in my nature. It's always so hard for me to not sort out an issue immediately.

At heart I am six years old and desperate for everyone to get along, desperate for resolution and peace.

Prior to our coaching, Raine used to shut down. I would have to wait for him to come around, while I was emotionally pacing. I would have to pause long enough for him to return to me, available to dive in—on his own time. That period for me is hell. I am a very quick responder, and so I had to learn that he isn't going anywhere. He just needs a minute, or an afternoon. I had to learn that that space away from him is okay. I had to fight the story in my head that he was off alone deciding that I was awful for him and that he would need to leave me, that he had made a terrible decision by loving me.

Over time there is a confidence built in love, in the foundation, if we just put in the work, if we put in the time and patience to *repair*. You begin to trust that you'll rise from the ashes if you do it enough times. That practice creates eventual peace in the body.

When Raine and I have a conflict and put this CPR into practice, it's incredible how efficiently things get sorted. We stick to the issue at hand, speak to the feelings, and don't turn the original problem into a runaway train and end up burning down the house.

But we are imperfect, and on that Sunday during the pandemic, I lit the torch and held it to the base of the curtains in our living room, ready to press it against the fabric.

Eventually we came back to each other from this incredibly intense place. Dr. John was able to help me to understand that enrolling our community in my problem only pours fuel on the fire and turns it into an all-consuming inferno, with its own weather system.

I was able to find Raine's perspective. Had he done something that hurt me? Sure. Was he not thinking of me? Sure. But I called our community, and I enlisted the kids, which I could only remember doing at one other point early in our relationship before we were parents.

MAMA BEAR

Before we became parents, we were young and in love and it was all feelings. At the beginning, you don't slow down to investigate why you were pulled to each other, you don't pre-emptively investigate all your baggage to make sure you are showing up as your best self. You just feel.

This is a beautiful stage, but it inevitably leads to issues down the road, when you realize to your great horror that you aren't naturally perfect for each other. It can become painful to face the reality that nobody is ever naturally perfect for each other all the time. We are constantly evolving and changing in response to invisible things past and present. It can take years of practice and coaching and mistakes to really investigate what is influencing behaviours. In some ways it's a miracle to me that we made it through those first few years.

My parents stayed together through everything; in that way, divorce never felt like it was on the list of possible menu items. Raine's parents did divorce, so even early on, it was available to order if you got hungry enough.

Raine and I were living in a loft on the corner of Queen and Claremont in Toronto, about three years into our relationship, just before we moved to LA. It was around this point that the little cracks in perfection began to reveal themselves. He had spent the bulk of a couple weeks turning a corner of the open concept space into a home studio. He ordered a bookshelf, in the hopes of creating the sensation of independence from the rest of the large single space.

The bookshelf arrived in five hundred pieces, the way Ikea shelves do. He was relentlessly frustrated as he laid out the sheets of paper and sorted the sack of screws into neat little piles on the hardwood floor. At one point he just snapped and yelled, "YOU WHORE."

Looking back, I am deeply aware that the derogatory slur was not meant for me. I imagine it was meant for the bookshelf, or the tiny easily misplaceable metal Allen key or maybe even for the founder of Ikea himself. But in the moment, I felt attacked. I had not been called a bad word since growing up as a teenager with my brothers. If that word was ever thrown around, I would be utterly gutted. Just hearing this word out of Raine's mouth made me see red. So I called his mom. She picked me up and I stayed the night at her place.

She made it very clear to me, some years back, that she was not my person when it came to conflicts with Raine. This may have been one of the greatest gifts ever given to me. I never wanted to discuss issues at home with my friends. I simply knew I was never leaving Raine, and I never wanted my friends to have any bad impressions of him, or be uncomfortable that we stayed together if they had a bad opinion of him. I certainly would never say anything bad about him to my parents because, well, they're my parents.

As a parent now, if my child said something in a bad light about their partner, I would naturally feel worried, concerned and primally protective, though I am confident I would have the patience and life experience to offer empathy on both sides. We are all human, and all of us are constantly and continually in a state of development. When it comes to partnering, it's a journey together. It has its ebbs and flows, its joy and its turmoil.

> "IT HAS ITS EBBS AND FLOWS, ITS JOY AND ITS TURMOIL."

These days, all three of our sons are in deep relationships, and I couldn't be happier for them. Despite the inevitable challenges that lie ahead, I trust that we have modelled loving partnership.

It's beautiful to observe our sons in this early *feeling* stage. Their coupling is only based on how they feel when they are together. They're ultimately choosing partners that bring them joy and comfort. It feels like a testament to Raine's and my hard work that our boys so effortlessly slip into the role of partner. It feels like the most powerful product of the work we have done to become better partners and individuals ourselves.

Our sons are way ahead of where Raine and I were in our teens. They have parents that we didn't have. They have parents who worked tirelessly to become cycle-breakers. They have been shown that asking for help is not a weakness, reaching out for professional guidance is a strength. This may be one of the most rewarding aspects of being a cycle-breaker, seeing your own children be better on a conscious and unconscious level. It's now in their DNA in a way that wasn't in ours.

But long before we became cycle-breakers, Raine's mom felt like the exact right place to put my pain, because Raine was never at risk of losing his own mother's love. When Raine's mom picked me up, I felt like she really helped me. It felt like I had enlisted necessary support in my case against Raine. He vowed he would never use language like that again, and he didn't.

When Raine's mom told me that she couldn't be my go-to person for grievances against her son, I had to find a real resolution to our problems. I no longer had my wing-woman for piling-on purposes.

Conflict resolution isn't about piling on and throwing fuel on a situation, thus exposing someone for the A-hole they are. It's not about pummelling them into submission. It's so much simpler. It's about connecting through conflict. It's about transforming a conflict into the potential for closeness.

We catch the problem—in this case, feeling attacked by the word "whore"—and we *pause*. By pausing, the partner hears the last thing they said ringing in their ear, and then, after a while, one or the other initiates *repair*. Repair is so important in these moments. Maybe the yelling and cursing we do when we're angry has so much to do with wanting to be heard. But how can we be heard when the situation itself feels chaotic? How do you catch the moment enough to stop the escalation?

When we pause and calm things, we come face to face with an opportunity to process. Momentum is a killer of processing. When we pause, we find the bravery to say, "Hey love, that fucking hurt me." And in that space the partner is hopefully able to access the opportunity to say, "Hey, I am so sorry, I recognize that was so not cool. It's not an excuse, but I hate Ikea, I was overwhelmed, and I blew a gasket. It hurts me that I would speak that way and I see how hurt you are. It won't happen again." It's so simple: recognize, validate, take responsibility, offer big hugs, kisses, wipe the tears, then go have some great sex.

Occasionally, I still call Raine's mom for advice or to get her perspective on something, but her son is never at the centre of my inquiry.

After the "whore" incident and long before we landed with Dr. John, Raine and I did go to someone else for counselling. It was somewhere near High Park, when we were still living in Toronto. We went in for a consultation. We did some kind of an "assessment," in which the counsellor listened to us a little, not much differently than John would some eight years later, and then offered us counselling—separation counselling.

I still can't believe it. I have heard experiences like this from devastated partners. It's like the counsellor doesn't want to get in and get their hands dirty, so they decide for you that it's over. Navigating the end must be so much cleaner than navigating staying. Perhaps they find the couple hopeless, so they let them know it's over and then offer themselves up as the expert to get them through the darkness and sadness and grief in a healthy and thoughtful way.

We looked at each other then looked at the counsellor, stood up and said, "Thank you for your time."

A bad therapeutic experience can halt the desire for help in its tracks. We wouldn't end up back in the pursuit of counselling for decades.

In a twisted sort of way, that therapist was exactly what we needed in that moment, because the simple threat of someone taking us away from each other was all we needed to be better.

After so many years together, the fact that we almost never swear or curse when things escalate is a miracle, and I think it's just a great rule for all couples. Words are like toothpaste; you can't put them back in the tube.

I believe that this is a key tool in our marriage. We have learned that it just doesn't work to pile past resentments onto each other, and we try to catch it quickly if we start slipping down into that hole of past resentments.

IKEA

Early in our relationship I found myself constantly ad-libbing when it came to conflict resolution. I'd never been taught how to read certain cues, mirror someone's feelings or validate them.

Like most young couples, we navigated a minefield of emotions. We were young and madly in love, so in general it was incredible, but I've always believed you only truly get to know yourself when a situation isn't easy. Challenges and how you deal with them tend to expose chinks in our armour. I certainly had a few.

There may be no greater challenge for a relationship than Ikea. Not the shopping aspect. Deciding how to furnish a shared space does come with the obvious challenges of compromise, but there is trauma waiting for you once you've left the giant parking lot.

Chantal and I had just finished our respective tours. We were finally going to be able to relax and spend some quality time in the super cool three-storey loft we'd just moved into. Tall windows and high ceilings were the exact opposite of living in a tour bus and travelling on airplanes and going from hotel to hotel. I felt a huge weight off my shoulders, knowing I didn't have to live out of a suitcase for a while.

We wanted to be minimalist, but we needed some storage stuff, a rug and a bathroom vanity. Why we drove all the way out to Ikea when we had ten amazing local furniture stores in our neighbourhood still irks me. My patience for massive stores like Ikea has always been limited, so we got out of there quickly with the specific items we needed—no meatballs.

Fast forward a few hours, and my mom was suddenly at our loft, standing over me as I slept on the couch, prodding me to wake up.

It was that damn bathroom unit.

It was a horror story. An engineer couldn't have put it together.

It took hours to work through that instruction booklet while trying to decipher the nuanced difference between different-size screws that looked no different to the naked eye.

Ikea should be a symbol for the stages of grief.

“IKEA SHOULD BE A SYMBOL FOR THE STAGES OF GRIEF.”

I was immediately shocked (stage one) with how complicated putting together a standing bathroom cabinet could be. This wasn't a bed or a dining-room table. It was a five-by-two-foot cabinet, and why didn't it just come assembled anyway?

I was not about to be intimidated: stage two, denial. As thick as that instruction manual was, I had grown up in the construction business and worked on construction sites. I sat on the floor in our bathroom surrounded by screws and wood pegs.

As I assembled the main frame, I started to feel like I wasn't given enough of those wood pegs to finish the cabinet. For a manual that was so precise, how could they possibly screw me on screws? The thought of having to drive back to Ikea was weighing on me as I searched the bathroom floor for more pegs. If the trauma of constructing this cabinet wasn't enough, Chantal was in the other room checking in with me throughout this process.

What started out as casual check-ins turned into judgments on my manhood. Not really, but frustration and the thought of imminent failure in front of my wife wasn't acceptable.

Was I able to be a provider? Was I able to take care of a partner?

This moved quickly to the anger phase, as I found myself now sweating, my legs cramping up as I sat on my knees looking for the right Allen wrench to fit the right screws.

The hours flew by, and what was supposed to be a nice evening at home turned into this bizarro life test.

The more Chantal inquired on my progress, the more stressful the situation became. Looking back, I'm sure it was meant half in fun and half the sincere desire to have a date night, but within the context of Ikea she began to get under my skin. This was one of my first domestic opportunities and failure was not an option, but after a few hours of feeling that Chantal was needling me, I snapped.

Out from my mouth, through the bathroom door into our living room where Chantal sat on our lounger, came a word I'd never thought I'd ever say. To anyone. If I'd used any other word, this would never have escalated to Chantal calling my mom in crisis. I'd never used this word before. I had Ikea syndrome and I called my just-married wife the C-word.

My maternal grandmother was from Manchester, and had that beautiful British, Oasis-style humour, but this wasn't that—or at least Chantal wasn't in on the joke. I slept on the couch that night, and a few hours later my mother was in my loft pushing on my shoulder begging me to wake up. Mortified her son could ever display such awful behaviour, she loomed over me.

The disappointment needed no words. The look in her eyes spoke volumes. Bad son.

She wasn't wrong.

Haven't been to Ikea since.

FIGHT OR FLIGHT

There is some scientific reasoning behind the concept that we are each other's healers, and for this the laws of attraction are based more on opposites.

Imagine that through some cosmic journey two people are picked to be together to heal each other, and the fact that you are somewhat opposing forces means you're destined to make each other better by drawing from different—or sometimes opposite—experiences.

In the case of Chantal and I, nothing could be more true. It's not hard to tell that I'm more introverted and that Chantal is definitely more of an extrovert. In more scientific terms, I'm a minimizer while she's a maximizer. This was new information to learn.

Chantal seeks emotional connection while I retreat. I'd never considered this before. These personality traits demonstrate how we adapt to stress differently. Our primitive brain must choose either fight or flight. I learned about this concept early on, when we were first dating. I was still living with my dad, and he'd just got a new ten-week-old retriever.

He'd also just moved into a new home, and the staircase going up to the second floor was varnished hardwood and supremely slippery. You were literally taking your life in your hands thinking you could navigate those stairs in a pair of socks.

One afternoon while Chantal and I were both in town and off the road, we were hanging out at my house and the new puppy ended up on the second floor. I was up there with her, and could tell she needed to go out. We were trying to train her.

In the panic of trying to not have to clean up pee, I forgot about the sock issue. Chantal was at the bottom of the stairs as I yelled for her to open the door, because the dog needed to go out in one dramatic step. While announcing this, my legs slipped out from under me. I began bouncing down the stairs on my ass and elbows, still holding the dog.

When my body finally rested about seven stairs down, I remember looking up at Chantal. Her eyes were as wide as saucers, and mouth open even wider. The look of shock on her face mirrored the look of shock on my face—except mine was trying to figure out if I'd broken anything, as I lay contorted halfway down the staircase.

In a million years I'd never have bet on what happened next. Chantal, without saying a word, ran away. We caught eyes for a second, and then she was gone. I slowly picked myself up, and as I made my way down the rest of the staircase and let the dog out, I searched for my girlfriend, who I was now thinking maybe wasn't "the one."

I can't even remember how she explained herself in that moment, and how I forgave her, but looking back it makes perfect sense. Our nervous systems are unique, and we are all susceptible to fight-or-flight instincts from our reptilian brains.

What's important to understand about these behaviours is that they are unconscious defence mechanisms—meaning they are deeply ingrained behaviours that have been programmed early on.

> "THE LOOK OF SHOCK ON HER FACE MIRRORED THE LOOK OF SHOCK ON MY FACE."

These aren't traits passed down from our parents or grandparents—they are physiological responses encoded in our DNA as survival tools.

It took a minute for me to get over her leaving me on that staircase. I was literally and figuratively butt-hurt. Her running away from that accident was her nervous system freaking out. Understanding that was big for me. There are countless examples, from early in our relationship, where knowing this reptilian brain part of humans would have been helpful. Luckily, we survived the stair incident and have become much better at stopping ourselves and stepping back from an emotional response, and understanding that the nervous system is not intentional.

I'M GOING TO BREAK YOUR HEART

Chantal heals from connection. No matter what has been said or however intense an argument has become, a simple touch or lean in from me means the world to her, and can heal in seconds. I love this about her. I see this resilience in our kids, the ability to come back so quickly from conflict is fascinating—especially coming from me, a self-admitted "work in progress."

I can go days without speaking after a conflict—or at least I used to be able to. It's that Italian thing where "I'm not mad" actually means "I'll never forget." If there's one thing I've become better at, it's forgetting. Don't get me wrong, the big things, I don't forget. But getting over most things quickly is a new, important gift.

We've managed to get to the point where Chantal and I can be in the middle of something quite intense and then, all of a sudden, we both start laughing, knowing how much of a waste of time it is to continue. In my view, when you get to this type of comfort and understanding with your partner, whether you had to spend a lot of money with professionals or whether it came naturally as a couple, you've found your soulmate.

The title "I'm Going to Break Your Heart," or at least my version of the meaning behind that song, is about being soulmates. It's also probably one if not the most romantic lyrics I've written—and that is not a sandbox I play in often.

The concept is based around the idea that once you fully commit to someone, beyond getting their name tattooed on your chest, once you have found your person or soulmate, the reality is that one of you will have their heart broken.

The heartbreak I'm speaking of has nothing to do with infidelity or walking out on your partner. It has nothing to do with letting your partner down emotionally, or not living up to some agreed-upon standard in the relationship. The heartbreak that the song was written about is as old as time itself. "I'm Going to Break Your Heart" is the reality that in true love, someone is bound to die first, thereby leaving the other heartbroken.

I felt this was some next-level *Romeo and Juliet* shit, until one day on stage, before performing the song to a packed theatre in Victoria, BC, I decided to explain a little behind the concept of the lyric.

For some reason I had always assumed Chantal and I were on the same page with this song, but after I told my version she grabbed her microphone and dismissed everything I'd just told the audience. This was a definite WTF moment.

Chantal's version contradicted mine from every angle. Her version, I learned that night on stage, was that every day we suffer, "little heartbreaks" as a couple. Up to twenty-five a day, she professed. *Kill me.* The idea of trying to heal a hundred heartbreaks a day is the least romantic thing I could ever think of.

On one hand I was surprised Chantal didn't back my romantic version of the lyric; but if I'm being real, I knew exactly where she was coming from, and it remains one of the few points of contention in our relationship.

The thing with marriage coaching or therapy is that it can be like drugs. You get the same euphoria and dopamine fix witnessing emotional connection and getting in your feelings with someone you love and trust, and with whom you ultimately want to spend your life with. It becomes addictive. It's not just the enlightened feelings or trust that is addictive, but it's also the actual work that's addictive.

It's something I've noticed since we started seeing Dr. John Grey. He's given us some amazing tools to combat all the different nuances of a relationship. The crazy thing is they all work, but you have to stick to the program, which means following the protocols exactly.

Take mirroring, for example. In any conflict resolution it's necessary to mirror someone's feelings of hurt or disrespect exactly. Too often we'd try this tactic, and Chantal would say, "Raine, when you told me you didn't want to play that song tonight without giving me a reason, I felt dismissed."

> "THE THING WITH MARRIAGE COACHING OR THERAPY IS THAT IT CAN BE LIKE DRUGS."

Trying to get through this conflict as quickly as possible, a typical response from me would be something like, "I'm sorry you felt bad when I didn't want to play that song."

This is not mirroring. The obvious part is that I didn't repeat her feelings word for word. You don't need to be a genius to understand that by skipping some words there is very little validating or healing about my approach. Point taken. And I've got much better at actual mirroring—and I'm alive today to say it truly works.

The issue is that having this happen a couple times a month is one thing, the idea of these little heartbreaks happening all day long and having to potentially address even a handful of those heartbreaks would drive any man—and potentially some women—absolutely mad. To be fair, Chantal has never gone to that extreme, but admitting that she has multiple heartbreaks a day is troubling because I believe in moderation. This applies to most things in my life, vices or not.

Moderation in the use of tools you've been given to build a healthy relationships is no different, in my book. The idea of constantly psychoanalyzing your relationship and being in the work ad nauseam could end up being worse than the conflict itself. This is why I was so troubled by Chantal's explanation for "I'm Going to Break Your Heart." I believe you can abuse the powers given to you to heal as a couple.

When I was growing up, my next-door neighbour, Will, was a car fanatic and was always working and restoring an old 1966 Chevelle. Every day after school, I'd hang out with Will while he was underneath that car fixing something. This restoration became famous in our neighbourhood, and we'd often have other local teens who had muscle cars or sports cars come by and do burnouts on the asphalt in front of Will's house.

It was almost a sign of respect for what was to come when Will finally unleashed this hot rod on Etobicoke. I remember thinking at one point in my twelve-year-old brain, "When is Will ever going to actually get this car on the road?"

I wondered if the satisfaction came more from working on the car, rather than actually ever driving it. I think the same applies to relationships, and the work needed to maintain and nurture healthy ones.

I guess I'm more of "let's go for a drive" guy, not someone who's constantly opening the hood and changing the oil. And this is a metaphor used by a guy who couldn't change the oil in an actual car if you paid me a million dollars.

THE CLICKER

There are two things that are almost always certain in my relationship with Raine: if we go out together, he drives, and when we watch TV, he has the clicker. While that may sound controlling, this dynamic works for us. Having Raine in the driver's seat allows me to be more easy-going about the journey itself; whereas if I am driving, we inevitably get into a scrap about one thing or another. When we are honest with ourselves, it allows us to be honest with each other. It allows us to accept within ourselves the desire to drive, the desire to be driven and to recognize both without judgment.

On this particular night, the clicker, as usual, was with Raine. What followed was entirely accidental, an easy and blameless incident. The clicker slipped out of his hand as he arched his arm in the air to more precisely connect with the cable box. It slipped, and fell directly, perfectly, onto my shin. While it wasn't a huge clicker, it fell on a part of the body without muscle or fat, just the thinnest layer of skin on top of the most surprisingly tender of bones.

I yelled, "Ow!" in the way you do when hit, in a way that is reactive and without punishment. It is only a response to a feeling. Something in my tone or my look as I said it made him feel attacked. And you know that old saying, "Attacked people attack people."

He responded reactively, a response to a feeling, "I didn't do anything!" This perceived attack followed by an instinctive defence started a cycle we know well. At this very moment the clicker ceased to exist. Everything that followed was distinctly not about the clicker. Suddenly it's, *Why can't he just say, "Are you OK?" Why can't he be concerned that I'm hurt?* But this argument is no longer about this argument at all. He is no longer him and I am no longer me. In a split second we are transformed, and his defensiveness contorts him into thinking I was lying about my pain. Lying as an opportunity to punish him. And I am searching for his empathy. I am searching for empathy in the face of my partner like I'm six and he is my father or brother.

Raine is an island man. His strength has been self-sustaining, protective. He has a life of building himself up to be strong, a one-man army that doesn't respond well to being responsible for someone else's well-being or pain and suffering. It's almost like there is a fear of empathy there. Like empathy will cause the walls he built for protection to fall down around him, leaving him vulnerable. This is a product of a lifetime of protecting oneself.

"THIS IS A PRODUCT OF A LIFETIME OF PROTECTING ONESELF."

There are times that we both manage to catch our reactivity, and when we do, our script looks really different. The moment I say, "Ow!" Raine catches it and he pauses and then says, "Are you OK? I'm sorry." Maybe he even kisses it better, maybe that leads to some intimacy, and we end up in the bedroom. That's obviously the best-case scenario.

It feels to me as though it's very hard to intervene on the ego, and so we slip into a shame-and-blame thing when we don't cut off this cycle before it begins. This is one of the many places where understanding each other's trauma from childhood is so valuable—to know each other's whys. Knowing your partner's *why* doesn't excuse shitty behaviour or unfair reactivity, but it can give the context required for patience. And patience inevitably leads to freedom.

I was raised in the church. Because of this, our vows included the reading of "Love is patient, love is kind." There are so many places that religion gets it so backwards, but this verse is just right. Love is slow. Love requires the patience to slow down, step outside of reactivity and connect with your partner.

HOW TO FIGHT

On the other side of our first intensive session with Dr. John, we have had years to face just how much coaching is not a quick fix. There is a sort of euphoria that can happen on the other side of a therapeutic breakthrough. It can, in moments, feel like you are forever healed. But inevitably the work continues. The point is the continued work. The coaching is merely an opportunity to strap new tools onto your leather belt to bring to work.

Fights are like rainbows. The definition and vibrancy is based on humidity, visibility, time of day—even where you're standing and when you notice one forming on the horizon.

A few days ago, I woke up and said to Raine, "Babe my feelings got hurt yesterday about something. Can we talk?" He dipped his head back, rolled his eyes, and for whatever reason this transpired:

RAINE: Oh God, what now?

On another day I may have received one of the following:

BETTER, SOMETIMES, RAINE: Oh God, what now? Sure. Give me a few minutes.

BETTER, AND MORE RARE, RAINE: Sure, let me just finish up this task.

BEST, BUT NOT THERE YET, RAINE: Absolutely my love. What's on your mind?

Nailing a response every single time is unrealistic and unsustainable. The thing that is sustainable is showing up, trying again, lifting your head up and heading back out there to give it another go.

I have been working so hard at this. When we get heated in our conversation as a couple, I try to remain neutral. I slow my words and soften my tone, curbing the animated nature of my voice to sound less reactionary and more matter of fact. I don't always manage to nail this, because nobody always nails anything. But when I do execute this technique well, the approach truly shifts the dynamic. In any dynamic we can't change others, or control them, but we can pivot ourselves.

The positive by-product of this self-awareness is that because our partner is a mirror, they will reflect that tone, or at least begin to. It's powerful. When I am able to step into conflict with my own nervous system calmed, he as a result is calmed too, and the world is a better place.

Raine doesn't want to be lectured, because, who does? But when I am clear and my words remain confident, I create far more space to receive criticism, direction. The more I am grounded in my own self-respect, the more open I am. And when I behave within my own patience and clarity when asking a question or making a demand, I name the rules of the game by abiding by them.

Humans are complex systems of baggage and triggers that can affect conflicts in different ways on different days. I am a feminist. I am fighting the patriarchy, on top of being triggered by my childhood traumas. I am fully loaded, like we all are. But conflicts are an opportunity to build trust, they are an opportunity to show up as each other's caregivers.

Raine is made up of his own specific cocktail of baggage and triggers that affect the way he shows up in conflict. He is a perfectionist. But the only job where he needs to continually strive for perfection is showing up, caring and validating my hurt. He doesn't have to believe he did anything intentionally.

The road to recovery is not claiming things that you don't believe to be true. The road to healthy conflict is, however, about sitting in the pain of the other, sharing in it, validating and empathizing with it even when you are unknowingly the cause of it.

He would never purposely try to hurt me. But his perfectionism stands in the way of just letting go in some moments. He naturally wants to be the perfect husband, so his instinct is to self-protect rather than sitting in a place of taking responsibility.

Now for the moustache dilemma. God, I hate a 'stache. I actually hate them. I'm honestly disappointed in myself that they have the power they have over me. The power to disgust and repel. I try so hard to be this high-frequency, heavily therapized, educated adult—and then a moustache on my man's face hijacks all my growth and I'm back at square one. I can't quite find the heart of this one. Maybe it's a sexual thing, I don't know. They just take me on a whole other journey in my mind, and I don't like it.

Needless to say, Raine is the most handsome guy I know. Like, I have hung out with a lot of celebrities. And Raine remains the most gorgeous—the only man I'm honestly attracted to. He is so sexy I can never get over it. But if he leaves that gentle strip of hair on his upper lip, something happens to me. Even the subtle moustache, that he says isn't a moustache, is enough to throw me into a highly animated, highly critical, fully reactionary state.

I recently posted a funny video on Instagram of Raine and I riding in the car. I stared at Raine, and he said, "Why are you looking at me like that?" I said, "Because of the moustache," and I followed it up with a cackle and the fans went wild. Raine laughed so hard from the moment that I posted it to Instagram, and everyone enjoyed the post. We were laughing together and reading people's comments. It was all in good fun.

Cut to two weeks later, we were at home battling the flu. Before bed, I looked over at him and I said, "Oh God, the 'stache is back," and he snapped. A perfect example of how with conflict, context is everything. Playing in the car with an audience is very different from being exhausted and sick in bed. Regardless, I don't love to be snapped at, so I turned around and went to sleep.

We don't believe in the old saying, "Don't go to sleep mad." Sometimes a good sleep and some space in your own head is exactly what you need to approach a conflict with a renewed sense of patience and direction.

In the morning, I had to get up regardless of being under the weather. When I next saw Raine, I absolutely could have chosen to go after him for how pissed he was at me for bringing up the 'stache while he was feeling sick and stressed out. I could have made it about his actions, but I didn't. I didn't say, "Sorry I upset you." Because that *still* makes it about the other person's reaction and responses. If I made it about my husband's feelings of hurt, he would deflect and offer a "I wasn't hurt . . ." Which would be my man's way of saying, "You hurt my feelings." Instead, I said, "Babe, I am sorry about bringing up the 'stache last evening." And he said, "That's okay, I love you."

> "THAT'S OKAY, BABE. I LOVE YOU."

This response from him was everything. It's perfect. A perfect set up from me, and a perfect response from him. It's in these moments that I want everyone to do the work, because the rewards run deep.

What's incredible is that I fell in love with him again in that moment. He didn't say, "Don't worry about it." He said, "That's okay, babe. I love you." Imagine if it had gone the other way and I made it about how prickly he was when he bit my head off. That version of this conversation looks very different.

Raine would have responded miffed, meeting combativeness with combativeness, "Are you serious right now? I have bronchitis, I am so stressed about breathing and having to get on a plane tomorrow and playing a show with the band for ten thousand people and all you can think about is my moustache and my temperament? This is twisted. You can't see how twisted this is?"

And he would have been right. Also, I would have been right for having my hurt feelings. Feelings are feelings—they're not wrong or right. But if I can hold his feelings and respect them, own my part and not deflect, tough as it is sometimes, that's the pattern I will eventually create. We are creating each other every single day.

STARTING SOMETHING

My memory is spotty after we left Sebastopol County and Dr. John after our first weekend intensive session, like my mind has decided what is important to keep. I can't remember the packing of our bags or the brushing of our teeth, the emptying of a fridge. It feels like the magnitude of the weekend overshadowed all of life's little inconsequential details, leaving only what is important to keep.

I remember the symphony of birds chirping in the woods as we walked out to the car, the light gently pouring through laced branches in the driveway. I don't remember what specifically I was wearing, but I can feel a floral printed dress, I can catch it out of the corner of my eye as I shut the car door.

I don't remember talking with Raine on the drive to the airport, but I remember laughing, hands woven together over a cup holder. He felt so light to me. I felt so light. It felt as if we had lifted hundreds of pounds of confusion and hopelessness up and off each other in those few days. The future was gorgeous again, within a renewed feeling of peace and possibility.

Leaving our retreat, I felt so connected to Raine, as though I could exhale and say anything without shame or insecurity or judgment. I knew we were truly a team and that nothing could come between us. I felt loved and seen and connected. It was back to how we felt when we were first together, without the stresses of kids and all the adulting that comes with marriage and family. It felt clear again, a renewed clarity, a youthful, playful, sexy, intimate truth—it was us against the world.

It's not like the weekend was a quick fix. Nothing is fixed overnight. Even now, I sometimes wonder how good we're actually doing. But I know for sure that without that weekend, without prioritizing the health of our relationship—learning and facing and sitting with the reality of each other—we would not be together today.

I must have emblazoned the feeling of that weekend somewhere in my mind and body because it has become a place to return to, a place of grounding, a place as essential to know as the edge of a cliff. It has become a place that offers me guideposts, showing me where the grass becomes mud, where the mud becomes a sheer rock face. It is now ingrained in me: where I can and should go *and* where I can't and should not go with my partner, even in the most difficult moments. Boundaries were set with scientific proof of who and why we are, and every day is a new opportunity to get it right or get it wrong and try again.

Entertainment. Writing. Culture.

ECW is a proudly independent, Canadian-owned book publisher. We know great writing can improve people's lives, and we're passionate about sharing original, exciting, and insightful writing across genres.

Thanks for reading along!

We want our books not just to sustain our imaginations, but to help construct a healthier, more just world, and so we've become a Certified B Corporation™, meaning we meet a high standard of social and environmental responsibility — and we're going to keep aiming higher. We believe books can drive change, but the way we make them can too.

Certified B Corporation
Learn more at bcorp.com

Being a B Corp means that the act of publishing this book should be a force for good — for the planet, for our communities, and for the people that worked to make this book. For example, everyone who worked on this book was paid at least a living wage. You can learn more at the Ontario Living Wage Network.

eBOUND DIGITAL CERTIFIED

This book is also available as an eBOUND Digital Certification (EDC) ebook. ECW Press's ebooks are screen reader friendly and are built to meet the needs of those who are unable to read standard print due to blindness, low vision, dyslexia, or a physical disability.

This book is printed on FSC®-certified paper. It contains recycled materials, and other controlled sources, is processed chlorine free, and is manufactured using biogas energy.

FSC
www.fsc.org
MIX
Paper | Supporting responsible forestry
FSC® C016245

ECW's office is situated on land that was the traditional territory of many nations including the Wendat, the Anishinaabeg, Haudenosaunee, Chippewa, Métis, and current treaty holders the Mississaugas of the Credit. In the 1880s, the land was developed as part of a growing community around St. Matthew's Anglican and other churches. Starting in the 1950s, our neighbourhood was transformed by immigrants fleeing the Vietnam War and Chinese Canadians dispossessed by the building of Nathan Phillips Square and the subsequent rise in real estate value in other Chinatowns. We are grateful to those who cared for the land before us and are proud to be working amidst this mix of cultures.

ecwpress.com